NGUI for Unity

Master NGUI components swiftly, and employ them to create a thrilling, action-packed 2D sci-fi game

Charles Bernardoff

PUBLISHING

BIRMINGHAM - MUMBAI

NGUI for Unity

First published: January 2014

Production Reference: 1170114

Published by Packt Publishing Ltd.
Livery Place
35 Livery Street
Birmingham B3 2PB, UK.

ISBN 978-1-78355-866-7

www.packtpub.com

Cover Image by Aniket Sawant (aniket_sawant_photography@hotmail.com)

Credits

Author
Charles Bernardoff

Reviewers
Adrián del Campo

Andreas Grech

Philip Pierce

Abdelrahman Saher

Acquisition Editor
Subho Gupta

Commissioning Editor
Shaon Basu

Technical Editors
Shubhangi H. Dhamgaye

Rohit Kumar Singh

Copy Editors
Roshni Banerjee

Aditya Nair

Shambhavi Pai

Project Coordinator
Joel Goveya

Proofreader
Simran Bhogal

Indexer
Hemangini Bari

Production Coordinator
Nitesh Thakur

Cover Work
Nitesh Thakur

About the Author

Charles Bernardoff has a bachelor's degree in Game Design and Level Design delivered by ISART Digital, a video games school located in Paris, France.

With four years of experience as game designer, level designer, and C# scripter at Cyanide Studio, Playsoft, and Airbus, Charles has worked on the PC versions of Blood Bowl, Dungeonbowl, and Confrontation. He has also worked on Unity and Flash mobile games, such as Space Run 3D, Oggy, and Psycho Gnomes.

He now works as Game Designer and Unity developer on PC and mobile Serious Games at Airbus.

I wish to personally thank Abdelrahman Saher, Usuario, and Andreas Grech, great reviewers who helped in making the book better. I also want to thank my family and friends for their great support while I was working on this project.

About the Reviewers

Adrián del Campo studied Computer Science at the Antonio de Nebrija University, specializing in server and DB administration. After a few years of working as a sysadmin and Java programmer, he decided to move to the game industry, pursuing a master's degree in Game Development at the Universidad Complutense. After that, he worked in top companies such as Pyro Studios and is currently working in Mediatonic Ltd. as a video game programmer. You can find him on twitter as @acampoh.

Andreas Grech is a Malta-based programmer and coffee aficionado. With over seven years of professional experience in the software development industry, he has worked on desktop applications, web experiences, and video games.

After earning his degrees from MCAST and the Fraunhofer-Gesellschaft and later working in Oslo, Norway, for a number of years, he settled back in Malta to start working in the video games industry, professionally with the Unity game engine.

Since then, Andreas has written a number of video games in Unity, including Typocalypse 3D, a web-based typing-shooter game, and No Photos, Please!, a local two-player stealth party video game. He also maintains a technical blog about his programming experiences at http://blog.dreasgrech.com.

Philip Pierce is a software developer with 20 years' experience in mobile, web, desktop, and server development; database design and management; and game development. His background includes creating AI for games and business software, converting AAA games between various platforms, developing multithreaded applications, and creating patented client/server communication technologies.

Philip has won several hackathons, including Best Mobile App at the AT&T Developer Summit 2013, and a runner-up for Best Windows 8 App at PayPal's Battlethon Miami. His most recent project was converting Rail Rush and Temple Run 2 from the Android platform to Arcade platforms.

Philip's portfolios can be found at `http://www.rocketgamesmobile.com` and `http://www.philippiercedeveloper.com`.

Abdelrahman Saher graduated with a B.Sc. in Computer Science in 2012. After graduation, Abdelrahman worked with the video game company Every1Plays, where he participated in the programming of a couple of mobile games. Later, in 2013, Abdelrahman moved into the challenging role of lead programmer with the video game company AppsInnovate. Apart from his work, Abdelrahman recently started his own start-up video game company, Robonite.

I would like to thank my family and friends for helping me and always being there for me.

www.PacktPub.com

Support files, eBooks, discount offers and more

You might want to visit www.PacktPub.com for support files and downloads related to your book.

Did you know that Packt offers eBook versions of every book published, with PDF and ePub files available? You can upgrade to the eBook version at www.PacktPub.com and as a print book customer, you are entitled to a discount on the eBook copy. Get in touch with us at service@packtpub.com for more details.

At www.PacktPub.com, you can also read a collection of free technical articles, sign up for a range of free newsletters and receive exclusive discounts and offers on Packt books and eBooks.

http://PacktLib.PacktPub.com

Do you need instant solutions to your IT questions? PacktLib is Packt's online digital book library. Here, you can access, read and search across Packt's entire library of books.

Why Subscribe?

- Fully searchable across every book published by Packt
- Copy and paste, print and bookmark content
- On demand and accessible via web browser

Free Access for Packt account holders

If you have an account with Packt at www.PacktPub.com, you can use this to access PacktLib today and view nine entirely free books. Simply use your login credentials for immediate access.

Table of Contents

Preface

This book is dedicated to beginners of the Next-Gen UI kit, also known as NGUI. You may have heard about this Unity 3D plugin; it is popular amongst developers for its easy-to-use and effective WYSIWYG workflow.

NGUI provides built-in components and scripts to create beautiful user interfaces for your projects, with most of the work happening inside the editor.

Through this book, you will gather the necessary knowledge to create interesting user interfaces. The seven chapters of this book are practical and will guide you through the creation of both a main menu and a 2D game.

What this book covers

Chapter 1, Getting Started with NGUI, describes NGUI's functionalities and workflow. We will then import the plugin and create our first UI system and study its structure.

Chapter 2, Creating Widgets, introduces us to our first widget and explains how we can configure it. It then explains how to create a main menu using the Widget template

Chapter 3, Enhancing Your UI, explains the drag-and-drop system and how to create draggable windows. It also covers the use of animations, scrollable text, and localization with NGUI.

Chapter 4, C# with NGUI, introduces C# event methods and advanced code-oriented components that will be used to create tool tips, notifications, and Tweens through code.

Chapter 5, Building a Scrollable Viewport, introduces us to an interactive fullscreen-scrolling viewport using scroll bars, keyboard arrows, and draggable items.

Chapter 6, Atlas and Font Customization, explains how you can customize your UI using your own sprites and fonts; this will enable us to modify the appearance of our entire main menu.

Chapter 7, Creating a Game with NGUI, covers game features, such as spawning mobile enemies, handling player input, and detecting collisions between widgets to create a game.

What you need for this book

In order to follow this book, you will need the Unity 3D software available at `http://unity3d.com/unity/download`.

You may use any version of Unity, but I recommend the 4.x cycle. Just the Add Component button and copy-paste component features will buy you some time. You must be familiar with Unity's basic workflow; the words GameObjects, Layers, and Components should not be a secret for you.

All the code pertaining to coding skills are available here and explained with comments on each line. So if you are not familiar with them, you will still be able to understand it.

While working with this book, we will create our own Sprites. If you do not want to or cannot create these assets by yourself, don't worry; the ones I have created for this book will be available for download.

You will also need the NGUI plugin for Unity by Tasharen Entertainment. You can buy it directly from the Unity Asset Store or you can click on the Buy Now button at the bottom of the page `http://www.tasharen.com/?page_id=140`.

Who this book is for

Whether you are a beginner starting to work with Unity 3D, an intermediate, or a professional developer searching for an effective UI solution, this book is for you.

You have worked on games or apps for PC, console, or mobile platforms, but are you struggling with Unity's built-in UI system to create your game's interfaces and menus? This is where you should be.

Once you have finished reading this book, you will discover that building a user interface can be easy, fast, and fun!

Conventions

In this book, you will find a number of styles of text that distinguish between different kinds of information. Here are some examples of these styles, and an explanation of their meaning.

Code words in text are shown as follows: "Declare a new `Difficulty` variable to store current difficulty."

A block of code is set as follows:

```
public void OnDifficultyChange()
{
  //If Difficulty changes to Normal, set Difficulties.Normal
  if(UIPopupList.current.value == "Normal")
    Difficulty = Difficulties.Normal;
  //Otherwise, set it to Hard
  else Difficulty = Difficulties.Hard;
}
```

When we wish to draw your attention to a particular part of a code block, the relevant lines or items are set in bold:

```
//We will need the Slider
UISlider slider;

void Awake ()
{
  //Get the Slider
  slider = GetComponent<UISlider>();
  //Set the Slider's value to last saved volume
  slider.value = NGUITools.soundVolume;
}
```

New terms and **important words** are shown in bold. Words that you see on the screen, in menus or dialog boxes for example, appear in the text like this: "You can now click on the **Create Your UI** button."

> Warnings or important notes appear in a box like this.

> Tips and tricks appear like this.

Reader feedback

Feedback from our readers is always welcome. Let us know what you think about this book—what you liked or may have disliked. Reader feedback is important for us to develop titles that you really get the most out of.

To send us general feedback, simply send an e-mail to feedback@packtpub.com, and mention the book title via the subject of your message.

If there is a topic that you have expertise in and you are interested in either writing or contributing to a book, see our author guide on www.packtpub.com/authors.

Customer support

Now that you are the proud owner of a Packt book, we have a number of things to help you to get the most from your purchase.

Downloading the example code

You can download the example code files for all Packt books you have purchased from your account at http://www.packtpub.com. If you purchased this book elsewhere, you can visit http://www.packtpub.com/support and register to have the files e-mailed directly to you.

Downloading the color images of this book

We also provide you a PDF file that has color images of the screenshots/diagrams used in this book. The color images will help you better understand the changes in the output. You can download this file from https://www.packtpub.com/sites/default/files/downloads/8667OT_ColorGraphics.pdf

Errata

Although we have taken every care to ensure the accuracy of our content, mistakes do happen. If you find a mistake in one of our books—maybe a mistake in the text or the code—we would be grateful if you would report this to us. By doing so, you can save other readers from frustration and help us improve subsequent versions of this book. If you find any errata, please report them by visiting http://www.packtpub.com/submit-errata, selecting your book, clicking on the **errata submission form** link, and entering the details of your errata. Once your errata are verified, your submission will be accepted and the errata will be uploaded on our website, or added to any list of existing errata, under the Errata section of that title. Any existing errata can be viewed by selecting your title from http://www.packtpub.com/support.

Piracy

Piracy of copyright material on the Internet is an ongoing problem across all media. At Packt, we take the protection of our copyright and licenses very seriously. If you come across any illegal copies of our works, in any form, on the Internet, please provide us with the location address or website name immediately so that we can pursue a remedy.

Please contact us at copyright@packtpub.com with a link to the suspected pirated material.

We appreciate your help in protecting our authors, and our ability to bring you valuable content.

Questions

You can contact us at questions@packtpub.com if you are having a problem with any aspect of the book, and we will do our best to address it.

1
Getting Started with NGUI

In this first chapter, we will talk about the overall workflow of NGUI before we import the plugin and create our first UI. Then we will look into the UI's structure, important parameters, and general behavior.

What is NGUI?

The **Next-Gen User Interface** kit is a plugin for Unity 3D. It has the great advantage of being easy to use, very powerful, and optimized compared to Unity's built-in GUI system, **UnityGUI**. Since it is written in C#, it is easily understandable and you may tweak it or add your own features, if necessary.

The **NGUI Standard License** costs $95. With this, you will have useful example scenes included. I recommend this license to start comfortably — a free evaluation version is available, but it is limited, outdated, and not recommended.

The **NGUI Professional License**, priced at $200, gives you access to NGUI's GIT repository to access the latest beta features and releases in advance.

A $2000 **Site License** is available for an unlimited number of developers within the same studio.

Let's have an overview of the main features of this plugin and see how they work.

UnityGUI versus NGUI

With Unity's GUI, you must create the entire UI in code by adding lines that display labels, textures, or any other UI element on the screen. These lines have to be written inside a special function, OnGUI(), that is called for every frame. This is no longer necessary; with NGUI, UI elements are simple GameObjects!

You can create widgets—this is what NGUI calls labels, sprites, input fields, and so on—move them, rotate them, and change their dimensions using handles or the Inspector. Copying, pasting, creating prefabs, and every other useful feature of Unity's workflow is also available.

These widgets are viewed by a camera and rendered on a layer that you can specify. Most of the parameters are accessible through Unity's Inspector, and you can see what your UI looks like directly in the Game window, without having to hit the Play button.

Atlases

Sprites and fonts are all contained in a large texture called atlas. With only a few clicks, you can easily create and edit your atlases. If you don't have any images to create your own UI assets, simple default atlases come with the plugin.

That system means that for a complex UI window composed of different textures and fonts, the same material and texture will be used when rendering. This results in only one draw call for the entire window. This, along with other optimizations, makes NGUI the perfect tool to work on mobile platforms.

Events

NGUI also comes with an easy-to-use event framework that is written in C#. The plugin comes with a large number of additional components that you can attach to GameObjects. These components can perform advanced tasks depending on which events are triggered: hover, click, input, and so on. Therefore, you may enhance your UI experience while keeping it simple to configure. Code less, get more!

Localization

NGUI comes with its own localization system, enabling you to easily set up and change your UI's language with the push of a button. All your strings are located in the .txt files: one file per language.

Shaders

Lighting, normal mapping, and refraction shaders are supported in NGUI, which can give you beautiful results. Clipping is also a shader-controlled feature with NGUI, used for showing or hiding specific areas of your UI.

We've now covered what NGUI's main features are, and how it can be useful to us as a plugin, and now it's time to import it inside Unity.

Importing NGUI

After buying the product from the Asset Store or getting the evaluation version, you have to download it. Perform the following steps to do so:

1. Create a new Unity project.
2. Navigate to **Window | Asset Store**. Select your download library.
3. Click on the **Download** button next to **NGUI: Next-Gen UI**.
4. When the download completes, click on the NGUI icon / product name in the library to access the product page.
5. Click on the **Import** button and wait for a pop-up window to appear.
6. Check the checkbox for **NGUI v.3.0.2.unitypackage** and click on **Import**.
7. In the Project view, navigate to **Assets | NGUI** and double-click on **NGUI v.3.0.2**.
8. A new imported pop-up window will appear. Click on **Import** again.
9. Click any button on the toolbar to refresh it. The NGUI tray will appear!

The NGUI tray will look like the following screenshot:

You have now successfully imported NGUI to your project. Let's create your first 2D UI.

Creating your UI

We will now create our first 2D user interface with NGUI's UI Wizard. This wizard will add all the elements needed for NGUI to work.

Before we continue, please save your scene as Menu.unity.

UI Wizard

Create your UI by opening the UI Wizard by navigating to **NGUI | Open | UI Wizard** from the toolbar. Let's now take a look at the UI Wizard window and its parameters.

Window

You should now have the following pop-up window with two parameters:

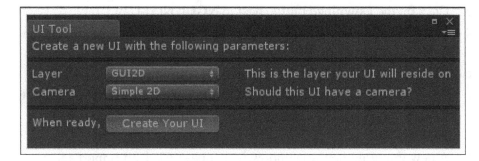

Parameters

The two parameters are as follows:

- **Layer**: This is the layer on which your UI will be displayed
- **Camera**: This will decide if the UI will have a camera, and its drop-down options are as follows:
  - ○ **None**: No camera will be created
  - ○ **Simple 2D**: Uses a camera with orthographic projection
  - ○ **Advanced 3D**: Uses a camera with perspective projection

Separate UI Layer

I recommend that you separate your UI from other usual layers. We should do it as shown in the following steps:

1. Click on the drop-down menu next to the **Layer** parameter.
2. Select **Add Layer**.
3. Create a new layer and name it GUI2D.
4. Go back to the UI Wizard window and select this new **GUI2D** layer for your UI.

You can now click on the **Create Your UI** button. Your first 2DUI has been created!

Your UI structure

The wizard has created four new GameObjects on the scene for us:

- UI Root (2D)
- Camera
- Anchor
- Panel

Let's now review each in detail.

UI Root (2D)

The **UIRoot** component scales widgets down to keep them at a manageable size. It is also responsible for the **Scaling Style** — it will either scale UI elements to remain pixel perfect or to occupy the same percentage of the screen, depending on the parameters you specify.

Select the **UI Root (2D)** GameObject in the Hierarchy. It has the UIRoot.cs script attached to it. This script adjusts the scale of the GameObject it's attached to in order to let you specify widget coordinates in pixels, instead of Unity units as shown in the following screenshot:

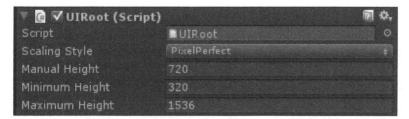

Parameters

The **UIRoot** component has four parameters:

- **Scaling Style**: The following are the available scaling styles:

    ◦ **PixelPerfect**: This will ensure that your UI will always try to remain at the same size in pixels, no matter what resolution. In this scaling mode, a 300 x 200 window will be huge on a 320 x 240 screen and tiny on a 1920 x 1080 screen. That also means that if you have a smaller resolution than your UI, it will be cropped.

    ◦ **FixedSize**: This will ensure that your UI will be proportionally resized depending on the screen's height. The result is that your UI will not be pixel perfect but will scale to fit the current screen size.

    ◦ **FixedSizeOnMobiles**: This will ensure fixed size on mobiles and pixel perfect everywhere else.

- **Manual Height**: With the **FixedSize** scaling style, the scale will be based on this height. If your screen's height goes over or under this value, it will be resized to be displayed identically while maintaining the aspect ratio (width/height proportional relationship).

- **Minimum Height**: With the **PixelPerfect** scaling style, this parameter defines the minimum height for the screen. If your screen height goes below this value, your UI will resize. It will be as if the **Scaling Style** parameter was set to **FixedSize** with **Manual Height** set to this value.

- **Maximum Height**: With the **PixelPerfect** scaling style, this parameter defines the maximum height for the screen. If your screen height goes over this value, your UI will resize. It will be as if the **Scaling Style** parameter was set to **FixedSize** with **Manual Height** set to this value.

 Please set the **Scaling Style** parameter to **FixedSize** with a **Manual Height** value of 1080. This will allow us to have the same UI on any screen size up to 1920 x 1080.

Even though the UI will look the same on different resolutions, the **aspect ratio** is still a problem since the rescale is based on the screen's height only. If you want to cover both 4:3 and 16:9 screens, your UI should not be too large—try to keep it square. Otherwise, your UI might be cropped on certain screen resolutions.

On the other hand, if you want a 16:9 UI, I recommend you force this aspect ratio only. Let's do it now for this project by performing the following steps:

1. Navigate to **Edit | Project Settings | Player**.
2. In the **Inspector** option, unfold the **Resolution and Presentation** group.
3. Unfold the **Supported Aspect Ratios** group.
4. Check only the **16:9** box.

Now that we have seen the UI Root's different parameters, let's discuss the camera.

Camera

Select the **Camera** GameObject in the **Hierarchy** view. It has the `UICamera.cs` script attached to it. This script must be attached to any camera that needs to interact with your UI.

Its purpose is to send different messages concerning events that happen to UI elements such as colliders attached to a button. Some of the more frequently used events are `OnClick()` and `OnHover()`.

You may have multiple cameras if you consider it necessary; for example, you can have an orthographic camera for 2D in-game UI elements and a separate perspective camera for a 3D pause menu.

For the purpose of this book, we will stick with only one camera.

Parameters

The `UICamera.cs` script has a large number of parameters as shown in the following screenshot:

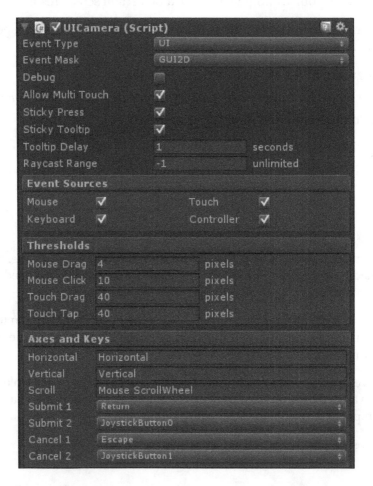

These parameters are as follows:

- **Event Type**: Select which event type this camera will send.
    - **World**: This is used for interacting with 3D-world GameObjects
    - **UI**: This is used for interacting with the 2D UI

- **Event Mask**: Select which layer will be used to receive events.
    - In our case, we will set it to **GUI2D** since our UI will reside on it.

- **Debug**: This consists of the enable or disable debug mode options. This option is useful when you have unwanted behavior.
  - ° Enabled: When **Debug** is enabled, the currently hovered object will be displayed on the top left-hand corner of the screen

- **Allow Multi Touch**: This consists of the enable or disable touch mode options that allow simultaneous touches. This is mandatory if you want to use pinch-to-zoom or other such gestures on mobile platforms.

- **Sticky Press**: This consists of the enable or disable sticky press mode options.
  - ° Enabled: If you drag your finger out of a pressed button, it will remain in the pressed state and no other element will receive upcoming events from that finger until it is released
  - ° Disabled: If you drag your finger out of a pressed button, it will no longer be pressed and other elements will receive upcoming events from that finger

- **Sticky Tooltip**: It consists of the enable or disable sticky tool tip mode options.
  - ° Enabled: The tool tip disappears when the mouse moves out of the widget
  - ° Disabled: The tool tip disappears as soon as the mouse moves

- **Tooltip Delay**: It consists of the required stationary time in seconds before the widget's tool tip is displayed.

- **Raycast Range**: A raycast is an invisible ray that is cast from one point towards a specific direction and is stopped if it encounters another object. The camera uses raycasts from the mouse or touch position towards the camera's forward direction to detect collisions and handle events. You may set the range of this raycast if you need to limit the interaction to a certain range. The default **-1** value implies that the raycast's range will be as far as the camera can see.

- **Event Sources**: These Booleans let you specify what events this camera listens to.
  - ° **Mouse**: This is used for mouse movements, left/right/middle click, and scroll wheel.
  - ° **Touch**: This is used for touch-enabled devices.
  - ° **Keyboard**: This is used for keyboard input. It uses the `OnKey()` event.
  - ° **Controller**: This is used for joystick-based devices. It uses the `OnKey()` event.

- **Thresholds**: These values come in handy when you want to specify the minimum values before a particular event is triggered. This may vary from one game/app to another.

    ○ **Mouse Drag**: When a mouse button is pressed (the OnPress() event is triggered), this value determines how far in pixels the mouse must move before it is considered a drag, and sends OnDrag() events to the dragged object

    ○ **Mouse Click**: When a mouse button is pressed (the OnPress() event is triggered), this value determines how far in pixels the mouse can travel before the button release has no effect (the OnClick() event is not triggered)

    ○ **Touch Drag**: This is the same as **Mouse Drag**, but for touch-based devices

    ○ **Touch Tap**: This is the same as **Mouse Click**, but for touch-based devices

- **Axes and Keys**: These parameters let you assign Unity input axes and keys to NGUI's input system.

    ○ **Horizontal**: This is the input axis for horizontal movement (the left and right key events)

    ○ **Vertical**: This is the input axis for vertical movement (the up and down key events)

    ○ **Scroll**: This is the input axis for scrolling

    ○ **Submit 1**: This is the primary keycode for validation

    ○ **Submit 2**: This is the secondary keycode for validation

    ○ **Cancel 1**: This is the primary keycode for cancel.

    ○ **Cancel 2**: This is the secondary keycode for cancel.

 You can edit Unity inputs at any time by navigating to **Edit | Project Settings | Input**.

Ok, we have seen what the main parameters of the UICamera component are. We have to see what the camera's anchor child is.

Anchor

An anchor is used to attach GameObjects to the same area inside the camera view. For example, you can attach them to borders or corners of the screen, or another widget.

Select the **Anchor** GameObject in the **Hierarchy** view. It has the **UIAnchor** component attached to it. It is configured to center content on the screen based on the parent camera.

Before we create widgets, we must understand how these **UIAnchor** parameters modify their placement behavior.

Parameters

The **UIAnchor** component has seven parameters as seen in the following screenshot:

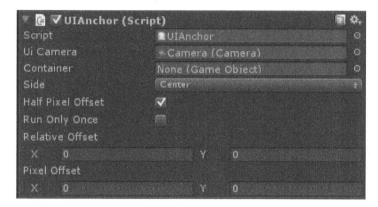

These parameters are as follows:

- **Ui Camera**: This is the reference camera from which our anchor bounds are determined. By default, it is set to the camera used by the UI.

- **Container**: If you drag and drop a GameObject in this field, it will overwrite the camera anchoring. This can be useful if you need to anchor your panels or widgets based on a container GameObject, instead of a camera. Your content will be placed using the assigned container's position.

- **Side**: Do you want your child GameObjects to be centered or attached to one side or corner of your referenced camera/container? You can choose your anchor point here.

- **Half Pixel Offset**: You should leave this Boolean checked. It makes widget positions pixel perfect on Windows machines.

- **Run Only Once**: This Boolean can be checked if your screen resolution never changes, or if you want it to remove it on start. As a result, your anchor will be executed at the start and then removed and no longer be updated.

- **Relative Offset**: This `Vector2` class takes two values between -1 and 1 to add a relative offset to the final position. With a value of 0.12 for **X** and 0.32 for **Y**, it will result in an offset of 12% horizontally and 32% vertically — it will look the same on any resolution because the offset depends on the screen size.

- **Pixel Offset**: This parameter is like **Relative Offset**, but it is absolute instead of relative. You can enter the offset in pixels — it will look different depending on the resolution because the offset will stay identical in pixels on all screen sizes.

We have explained the different **UIAnchor** parameters, but what is this last child, Panel? Let's look into that, and we'll be ready to create our first widget!

Panel

Select the **Panel** GameObject in the **Hierarchy** view. It has a **UIPanel** component attached.

A panel's purpose is to hold widgets and render geometry in only one draw call. You may create multiple panels to split your UI, but it will add a draw call per new panel.

Parameters

The `UIPanel.cs` script has eight parameters as shown in the following screenshot:

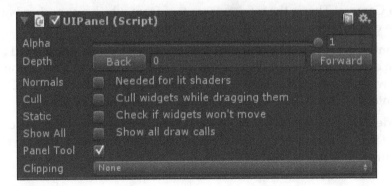

These parameters are as follows:

- **Alpha**: You may change the **transparency level** of the entire panel. All child widgets will be affected by this alpha value, but nested panels won't.

- **Depth**: This is used to define which panel is rendered over another. A panel with a depth value of 1 will appear in front of a panel with a depth value of 0. You can use either the **Back** or **Forward** button to change the **Depth** or simply enter a number in the field. Panels can also have negative depth.

- **Normals**: This Boolean must be checked if you need it to react to lighting using shaders. It will calculate normals for your UI geometry.

- **Cull**: This Boolean gives you the ability to disable the child widgets rendering while the panel is being dragged, which improves performance.

- **Static**: If all your panel's widgets are static and won't ever move, check this—it will improve performance!

- **Show All**: This will show all draw calls in the **Inspector** view.

- **Panel Tool**: This is a panel managing tool. You can visualize and select each panel in the scene. You can open it with *Alt + Shift + P* or navigate to **NGUI | Open | Panel Tool**. Will this panel show in the **Panel Tool** parameter? This should be unchecked for dynamically created temporary panels through code, like a warning message or ammo pick-up notification.

- **Clipping**: This will let us hide widgets outside a given rectangle. When turned on, you will be able to choose the clipping rectangle's dimensions with the `Center` and `Size` parameters. Anything outside this rectangle will be hidden.

  - **None**: No clipping—the entire panel will be displayed.
  - **Hard Clip**: Clipping enabled—rough clipping of widgets outside the box.
  - **Soft Alpha**: Clipping enabled—soft clipping with fade-out / fade-in borders.

We've now taken a look at the parameters of the **UIPanel** component, which will be used to hold our widgets.

Summary

During this chapter, we discussed NGUI's basic workflow—it works with GameObjects, uses atlases to combine multiple textures in one large texture, has an event system, can use shaders, and has a localization system.

After importing the NGUI plugin, we created our first 2D UI with the UI Wizard, reviewed its parameters, and created our own GUI 2D layer for our UI to reside on.

Finally, we analyzed the four GameObjects that were created automatically for us by NGUI. After reviewing their parameters, we can summarize their roles as follows:

- The **UI Root** holds the UI and scales it for pixel perfect or fixed sizes
- The **Camera** views the UI and sends messages to the widgets for interactions
- The **Anchor** can attach elements to the borders of screen or objects and add offsets
- The **Panel** holds our widgets and renders them, with or without clipping

We are now ready to create our first widget. It's time to move on to the next chapter.

2
Creating Widgets

In this chapter, we will create our first sprite widget and understand how it works. Then we will create one sample of each important widget template, and analyze their corresponding parameters so that you know how to create and configure them.

At the end of this chapter, we will have a functional main menu with most of NGUI's widgets.

Creating our first widget

We will create our first sprite widget to display our main menu's background window. In order to do that easily, NGUI has a **Widget Wizard** with a few templates for us.

Widget Wizard

The Widget Wizard can be opened by navigating to **NGUI | Open | Widget Wizard**. It will look like the following screenshot:

As you can see in the previous screenshot, to create a widget, you require **Atlas** and **Font** to be configured. As said in *Chapter 1, Getting Started with NGUI*, an atlas is a large texture containing the sprites that you need to create your UI. For the rest of this chapter, we will use the default atlas named **SciFi Atlas**, which is included in the plugin.

Selecting an atlas

Let's select our default SciFi atlas, which contains the necessary sprites, as follows:

1. In the **Project** view, navigate to **Assets | NGUI | Examples | Atlases | SciFi**.
2. Drag-and-drop the prefab `SciFi Atlas.prefab` in the **Atlas** field.
3. Drag-and-drop the prefab `SciFi Font - Header.prefab` in the **Font** field.

We have our **Atlas** and **Font** prefabs selected. We can now create a widget from a template.

Creating a widget from a template

Let's create a widget from a template by performing the following steps:

1. Click on the drop-down menu next to the **Template** field.
2. Select the **Sprite** option as **Template**.
3. Click on the drop-down menu next to the **Sprite** field.
4. Select the sprite named **Dark**.
5. Leave the **Pivot** option as **Center**.
6. Make sure you have selected **Panel** in the **Hierarchy** view.
7. Click on the **Add To** button.

Ok, our sprite widget has been created!

> The widget wizard adds the new widget as the child of the selected GameObject or panel. If you have selected the wrong GameObject, you can still drag-and-drop the new widget into the right GameObject after it is created.

Transforming widgets

We have created our first widget: **Sprite (Dark)**. Select it in the **Hierarchy** view and try the following manipulations to change its transform values.

Moving widgets

In the **Scene** view, you can use the **handles** to move your widget or you may enter coordinates directly in the **Inspector** view's **X**, **Y**, or **Z** parameters. The following screenshot is of the **Scene** view with the three parameters visible:

You should always leave the **Z** coordinates at 0. If you need to place a widget behind or in front of another, use the **Back** and **Forward** buttons in the **Inspector** view to control your widget's depth.

> You may move your widget on only one axis by pressing *Shift* before you click on the axis's handle.

Rotating widgets

On the **Scene** view, place your mouse cursor on the outside of any blue circle surrounding your widget. Your cursor will have a rotation icon next to it. You can now keep your left mouse button pressed and move your mouse to rotate the widget.

By default, rotation is set to have a 15 degrees step. If you wish to have a more precise rotation—a 1 degree step—just hold *Shift* while rotating.

Scaling widgets

You may have noticed that in the **Inspector** view, the scale value is grayed out. That's because you should use the **Dimensions** parameter of the **UISprite** component instead.

On the **Scene** view, place your mouse cursor on any blue circle surrounding your widget. Your cursor will have a resize icon next to it. You can now click and drag your mouse to resize the widget.

 Using the blue handles will *not* keep your widget centered to its current position. If you want to resize your widget proportionally on both sides, click on the space in front of the **X** or **Y** parameter of **Dimensions** of the **UISprite** component and drag your mouse left or right.

To keep everything pixel perfect, you should avoid scaling widgets up or down with Unity's scale tool. Try to do everything with **Dimensions**. Let's see what other parameters we have for widgets.

Common widget parameters

Select **Sprite (Dark)** and you will find the parameters seen in the following screenshot in the **Inspector** view:

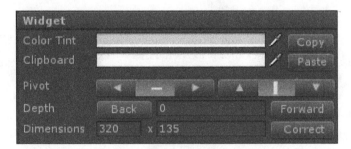

These parameters exist for any type of widget. Let's see what they are:

- **Color Tint**: This is the widget's alpha-enabled color.
- **Clipboard**: If you click on the **Copy** button, the current **Color Tint** selection is copied to this parameter. If you click on the **Paste** button, the **Clipboard** parameter's selection will be pasted to **Color Tint**.
- **Pivot**: This presents two sets of buttons that can be used to choose which corner or side you want the widget's pivot to be placed.
- **Depth**: This can be used to display your widget in front or behind others.
- **Dimensions**: This can be used to display size in pixels instead of scaling.

Now that we have seen the widget parameters, please enter these **Dimensions** for our newly created **Sprite (Dark)**: 1300 x 850.

Our sprite window just got enormous and ugly. Why? Because it's a 15 x 15 sprite stretched to 1300 x 850! Let's talk about sprites and see how we can correct this.

Sprites

We have created our first sprite and understood how to move, rotate, and change its dimensions. We actually scaled it up massively compared to its original size. But this 15 x 15 sprite has something special.

If you select the **Sprite (Dark)** GameObject, you will see it has four dotted lines inside the **Preview** window in the **Inspector** view. This means it's a **sliced sprite**:

Sliced sprites

A **sliced** sprite is an image divided in nine sections, making it resizable while conserving its corners' proportions. Sliced sprites may be scaled as you wish — they still look beautiful.

Since **Sprite (Dark)** is a 9-slice sprite, we must tell our **UISprite** component to treat it as such. Perform the following steps to do so:

1. Select the **Sprite (Dark)** GameObject.

2. Click on the drop-down menu next to its **Sprite Type** field.

3. Select **Sliced**.

Notice how the sprite looks good now — it's not stretched anymore!

> The **Fill Center** parameter allows you to only show the sprite's borders and leave only transparency inside.
>
> Even though sliced sprites are perfect for windows and variable size boxes, you may display regular sprites by leaving **Sprite Type** as **Simple**.

Tiled sprites

A tiling sprite is a pattern meant to be repeated indefinitely — it can be used to cover a large surface by repeating the same texture. Let's try it right now:

1. In the **Hierarchy** view, rename **Sprite (Dark)** as Window.

2. Select our **Window** GameObject and perform the following steps:

    1. Make sure it is at {0, 0, 0} position and has a scale of {1, 1, 1}.

    2. Make sure **Depth** is set to 0.

    3. In the **Color Tint** parameter, change **R** to 115, **G** to 240, **B** to 255, and **A** to 255.

Ok, we have our window. Let's create a tiled background to make it look better by performing the following steps:

1. Select our **Window** GameObject and duplicate it with *Ctrl + D*.

2. Rename the duplicate as Background.

3. Select the new **Background** GameObject and perform the following steps:

   1. Set its UISprite's **Depth** parameter to 1.

   2. Click on the drop-down menu next to the **Sprite Type** field.

   3. Select **Tiled**. It doesn't look good because our sprite is not a tiling sprite.

   4. Click on the **Sprite** button.

   5. Select the **Honeycomb** sprite, which is a tiling sprite.

   6. In the **Color Tint** parameter, change **R** to 115, **G** to 240, **B** to 255, and **A** to 255.

4. Attach a component to it by navigating to **Component | NGUI | UI | Stretch** and perform the following steps:

   1. Drag-and-drop our **Window** GameObject inside the **Container** field.

   2. Set the **Style** field to **Both**.

5. Attach a component to it by navigating to **NGUI | Attach | Anchor** and drag-and-drop our **Window** GameObject inside the **Container** field.

That looks better! We now have a tiling sprite for our window's background, and it looks as follows:

We used the **UIStretch** component to avoid setting dimensions manually; if you change the window's **Dimensions**, the background will resize itself automatically.

The **UIAnchor** component is used to make sure the background also moves with the window.

Filled sprites

A filled sprite is useful to create life bars or progress bars; with this, you can set a sprite and change the **Fill Amount** parameter between 0 and 1 to hide a part of it. The following screenshot shows a partially hidden progress bar:

Let's create this effect with the following steps:

1. Select our **Background** GameObject and set **Sprite Type** to **Filled**.
2. Set **Fill Dir** to **Horizontal**.

Move the **Fill Amount** slider and you can see what it does on the game view. You've understood the filled sprite system. Now set the **Sprite Type** field back to **Tiled**.

Ok, we've seen different sprite widgets and parameters. Let's learn how to add text.

Labels

Labels are used to display text on the screen with a specific font as shown in the following screenshot:

Let's create a label widget with the following steps:

1. Select the **Panel** GameObject.
2. Navigate to **NGUI | Open | Widget Wizard**.
3. Select the **Label** template.
4. We have already selected a font; it will be used for this label.
5. Click on the **Add To** button.

A new label has been added to the panel and placed at the center of the screen.

Parameters

With **Label** selected, the UILabel parameters are shown in the **Inspector** view. They are as follows:

- **Text**: This is a large textbox that lets you type the text to be displayed.
- **Overflow**: This offers four different behaviors for the widget when the text is larger than the label's **Dimensions**. The four behaviors are as follows:
    - **Shrink Content**: This shrinks the text in order to fit
    - **Clamp Content**: This ensures overflow will never happen
    - **Resize Freely**: This resizes to display all the content and overflow
    - **Resize Height**: This resizes height only — column style
- **Encoding**: This must be checked if you want to change the characters' color by inserting the [RRGGBB] hexadecimal values.
- **Effect**: This will help you add a shadow or outline effect to your label. You can adjust the **Distance** and **Color** values.
- **Max Lines**: This is the maximum number of lines assigned for the label. For unlimited lines, leave it as **0**.
- **Pivot**: The pivot also defines how the text is aligned.

Creating the title bar

Let's add a title for our window that will look like the following screenshot:

Please proceed with the following steps to create this title bar for our window:

1. Select **Panel** and create a new child with *Alt + Shift + N*.
2. Rename that new child as Title. It will be our Title bar container.
3. Drag-and-drop the **Label** GameObject into the **Title** GameObject.
4. Select our **Title** GameObject.
5. Navigate to **NGUI | Open | Widget Wizard**.

6. Create a new sprite using the **Highlight** sprite and perform the following steps:

   1. Rename this new sprite (**Highlight**) as `Background`.
   2. Set **Sprite Type** to **Sliced**.
   3. Change the **Pivot** option to **Top** (the button with the up arrow).
   4. Reset its **Transform** position to {0, 0, 0}.
   5. In the **Color Tint** parameter, change **R** to 95, **G** to 255, **B** to 150, and **A** to 200.
   6. Enter **Depth** as 2.

7. Attach a component to it by navigating to **Component | NGUI | UI | Stretch** and perform the following steps:

   1. Drag our **Window** GameObject into the **Container** field.
   2. Set **Style** to **Horizontal**.
   3. Enter its UISprite's **Y** dimension as 62.

8. Select the **Label** GameObject from **Title** and perform the following steps:

   1. Change its text to [AAFFFF]Main Menu.
   2. Set its **Overflow** parameter to **Resize Freely**.
   3. Enter **Depth** as 3.

9. Attach a component to it by navigating to **NGUI | Attach | Anchor** and perform the following steps:

   1. Drag-and-drop the **Background** GameObject from **Title** in the **Container** field.
   2. Set the **Side** parameter to **Center**.

10. Select our **Title** GameObject in the **Hierarchy** view.

11. Attach a component to it by navigating to **NGUI | Attach | Anchor** and perform the following steps:

    1. Drag our **Window** GameObject into the **Container** field.
    2. Set the **Side** parameter to **Top**.

The **Hierarchy** and **Inspector** views of our **Title** GameObject should look like the ones in the following screenshot:

We now have a window that actually looks like a window. We used anchors to avoid setting positions manually. Now let's add some buttons!

Buttons

With NGUI, buttons are easy to create and configure.

Let's create our first one by performing the following steps:

1. Select the **Panel** GameObject.
2. Create a new child with *Alt + Shift + N* and perform the following steps:
    1. Rename it as Buttons. It will be our buttons container.
3. Navigate to **NGUI | Open | Widget Wizard** and perform the following steps:
    1. Select the **Button** Template.
    2. For the **Background** field, select the sprite named **Button**.
4. With the **Buttons** GameObject selected, click on the **Add To** button.

A button has just been created and centered on the screen. If you look at the **Hierarchy** view, you will see that a button is composed of a container GameObject named **Button** and two children: a **Background** sprite and **Label**. That's how NGUI works; templates are simply assembled components and widgets. If you wanted to, you could build a button from scratch using the right components on empty GameObjects.

Click on the Play button. You can see that hover and click are already set! Turn off the Play mode, select the new **Button** GameObject, and look at the **Inspector** view.

Interactive widgets have a box collider attached to them, and that is the case with this button. The collider is used to detect collisions with the cursor.

Parameters

A button has a UIButton component that handles seven button parameters:

- **Target**: This GameObject is transformed and modified when the user hovers or presses the button. By default, this is **Background**.
- **Normal**: This is the color tint when nothing is happening.
- **Hover**: This is the color tint when the user's cursor is over the button.
- **Pressed**: This is the color tint when the user clicks on the button.
- **Disabled**: This is the color tint when the button is disabled (can't be clicked).
- **Duration**: This is the duration of transitions between states.
- **Notify**: This is the parameter that lets you choose a method to call when the button is clicked. You must first drag a GameObject into the **Notify** field. A **Method** field will then appear, listing the GameObject's attached script methods, as shown in the following screenshot:

In the previous example, I dragged the **Panel** GameObject into the **Notify** field. My **Panel** GameObject has a ButtonManager.cs script attached to it—this script has a ButtonClicked() method. I can now select it in the **Method** field. It will be called on click.

Only **public** methods without arguments will show in the **Method** field of the **Notify** parameter.

There is also a **PlaySound** component attached to this button. It lets you choose an audio clip to play when the selected event occurs. You can edit the **Pitch** and **Volume** parameters.

 You can add as many **PlaySound** components as you want if you need a sound to be played whenever the user hovers or clicks on something, for example.

The play and exit buttons

We will now add two buttons to our window that will exit or launch the game. They will appear as shown in the following screenshot:

We need a GameObject that will manage the game. It will contain the GameManager.cs script attached in order to manage generic behaviors such as exiting or launching the game. Let's create it first; follow these steps to do so:

1. Create a new GameObject at the root of **Hierarchy** with *Ctlr + Shift + N* and perform the following steps:

    1. Rename it as GameManager.

2. Create and attach a new GameManager.cs C# script to it and perform the following steps:

    1. Open this new GameManager.cs script.

    2. Inside this new script, add this new method called ExitPressed() with the following code lines:

       ```
       public void ExitPressed()
       {
         //Exit Now
         Application.Quit();
       }
       ```

Now that the exit method is ready, let's create and configure the two buttons as shown in the following steps:

1. Select the **Button** GameObject and perform the following steps:
   1. Rename it as Exit.
   2. Drag the **GameManager** GameObject into the **Notify** field.
   3. Choose **GameManager.ExitPressed** in the **Method** field.
   4. In the **Normal** color tint parameter, change **R** to 185, **G** to 255, **B** to 255, and **A** to 255.
   5. In the **Hover** color tint parameter, change **R** to 0, **G** to 220, **B** to 255, and **A** to 255.

2. Attach a component to it by navigating to **NGUI | Attach | Anchor** and perform the following steps:
   1. Drag our **Window** GameObject into the **Container** field.
   2. Set the **Side** parameter to **BottomLeft**.
   3. Set **Pixel Offset** to {135, 60}.

3. Select our **Exit** button's child **Background** GameObject and perform the following steps:
   1. Enter **Depth** as 2.

4. Select our **Exit** button's child **Label** GameObject and perform the following steps:
   1. Change its text to Exit.
   2. Enter **Depth** as 3.

Ok, we have our **Exit** button. Let's create our **Play** button as follows:

1. Duplicate the **Exit** button and perform the following steps:

    1. Rename this new duplicate as `Play`.

    2. Click on the **Minus** button next to the UIButton's **Notify** field to remove the **GameManager** GameObject from it.

    3. Set its **Side** parameter to **BottomRight**.

    4. Set **Pixel Offset** to {`-135, 60`}.

2. Attach a Component to it by navigating to **Component | NGUI | Examples | Load Level On Click**, and set its **Level Name** string parameter to **Game**.

3. Select our **Play** button's child **Label** GameObject, and change its text to `Play`.

Perfect, now if you build your scene, you will have a functional **Exit** button with only one line of code! The **Pixel Offset** parameter maintains our buttons at the same distance from the window's borders even if you change resolutions or the window's dimensions. We will create our game scene later.

> **Image buttons** can also be created with the Widget Wizard. They are identical to normal buttons, except that they use images for the **Normal**, **Hover**, **Pressed**, and **Disabled** states instead of color and scale tweens.

Text input

Now we will learn how to add a text input to create a nickname box. Perform the following steps to do so:

1. Select the **Panel** GameObject and create a new child with *Alt + Shift + N*. Then rename this new child as `Nickname`. It will be our nickname box container.

2. Navigate to **NGUI | Open | Widget Wizard**.

    1. From the **Project** view, navigate to **NGUI | Examples | Atlases | SciFi**.

    2. Drag the **SciFi Font – Normal** prefab into the **Font** field.

    3. Select the **Input** template.

    4. Set **Sprite (Dark)** as the **Background** parameter.

3. With the **Nickname** GameObject selected, click on the **Add To** button.

A new widget named **Input** has been added to the scene.

Parameters

An **Input** GameObject has been created. Let's look at its **Inspector** parameters:

- **Input Label**: This is the text label that is to be used for this input.
- **Inactive Color**: This is the text color while the text is not selected.
- **Active Color**: This is the text color while the text is being edited.
- **Default Text**: This is either **Blank** or with the label's default text. **Blank** will delete the label's text when the **Input** GameObject is selected.
- **Keyboard Type**: This allows the different sets of characters to be authorized. This will also change the keyboard layout on mobile platforms.
- **Select on Tab**: Drag into this field the GameObject that you want to be selected when the *Tab* key is pressed while editing the input.
- **Auto-save Key**: This enables the label's text to be automatically saved to the specified `PlayerPrefs()` key.
- **Max Characters**: This is the number of maximum characters allowed. `0` means infinite.
- **Carat Character**: This is the end of text character.
- **Password**: If you activate this Boolean, the label's characters will be replaced by * on the screen.
- **Auto-correct**: This enables or disables autocorrection on mobile platforms.

Creating a nickname box

Let's use this text input to create a nickname box that will look like the following screenshot:

Let's create the nickname box seen in the preceding screenshot.
Perform the following steps to do so:

1. Duplicate the **Window** GameObject and perform the following steps:
    1. Rename the new duplicate as `Background`.
    2. Drag it into the **Nickname** container GameObject.
    3. Enter **Depth** as `2`.
    4. Set **Dimensions** to `440 x 120`.

2. Select our **Input** GameObject and perform the following steps:

    1. Reset its **Box Collider** component's center to {0, 0, 0}.

    2. Type in `Nickname` for the **Auto-save Key** parameter.

    3. Enter **Max Characters** as 25.

3. Attach a component to it by navigating to **NGUI | Attach | Anchor** and perform the following steps:

    1. Drag the **Background** GameObject from **Nickname** inside the **Container** field.

    2. Set the **Pixel Offset** to {0, -17}.

4. Duplicate the **Label** child GameObject from **Title** and perform the following steps:

    1. Drag it inside the **Nickname** GameObject.

    2. Change its text to `[AAFFFF]Nickname`.

    3. Drag the **Background** GameObject from **Nickname** inside the **Container** field.

    4. Set the **Side** parameter to **Top**.

    5. Set **Pixel Offset** to {0, -32}.

5. Select the **Background** child GameObject from **Input** and perform the following steps:

    1. Enter **Depth** as 3.

    2. Set **Pivot** to **Center** (middle button + middle button).

    3. Reset the **Transform** field's position to {0, 0, 0}.

    4. In the **Color Tint** parameter, change **R** to 100, **G** to 230, **B** to 255, and **A** to 255.

6. Select the **Label** child GameObject from **Input** and perform the following steps:

    1. Enter **Depth** as 4.

    2. Set **Pivot** to **Center** (middle button + middle button).

    3. Reset the **Transform** field's position to {0, 0, 0}.

    4. Change the **Label** GameObject's text to `Enter your Name Here`.

7. Select the **Nickname** container GameObject.

8. Attach a component to it and navigate to **NGUI | Attach | Anchor** and perform the following steps:

   1. Drag-and-drop our **Window** GameObject inside the **Container** field.

   2. Set the **Side** parameter to **Top**.

   3. Set **Pixel Offset** to {0, -220}.

Ok, we have a **Nickname** box. Your **Hierarchy** view should look like the following screenshot:

The user can enter his nickname, up to 25 characters. If you move or change the window's dimensions, our box will move to stay at the same place.

Slider

Now let's add a volume slider for the user to move and select his/her volume level.

A slider template is available, enabling you to adjust parameters easily by sliding a thumb along a bar. Perform the following steps to create a volume slider:

1. Select the **Panel** GameObject and create a new child with *Alt + Shift + N*.

2. Rename that new child as Volume. It will be our volume settings container.

3. Navigate to **NGUI | Open | Widget Wizard** and perform the following steps:

   1. Select the **Slider** template.

   2. Set the **Dark** Sprite to **Empty**.

   3. Set the **Light** Sprite to **Full**.

   4. Set **Highlight** to **Thumb**.

4. With the **Volume** GameObject selected, click on the **Add To** button.

Parameters

A slider has been created. It has 6 parameters as follows:

- **Value**: This is the slider's current value, which is between 0 and 1.
- **Steps**: This is the number of steps to completely fill or empty the slider.
- **Direction**: This is the slider's fill direction, either **Horizontal** or **Vertical**.
- **Foreground**: This is the sprite used to fill the slider.
- **Thumb**: This is the sprite used for the handle to change the slider's value. By leaving this as **null**, a simple progress bar will be created (user cannot interact).
- **Notify**: This is the GameObject that lets you choose a method to call when there is a change in the slider's value. When a GameObject is assigned, you may choose a method to call on the value change.

Creating a volume slider

We can use this slider to create our volume slider, which will look like the following screenshot:

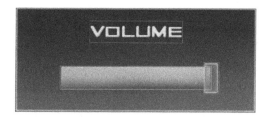

Proceed with the following steps to create it:

1. Duplicate the **Background** GameObject from **Nickname** and perform the following steps:
    1. Drag the duplicate inside the **Volume** container GameObject.
    2. Set its **Dimensions** to 320 x 135.

2. Attach a component to it by navigating to **NGUI | Attach | Anchor** and perform the following steps:
    1. Drag our **Window** GameObject inside the **Container** field.
    2. Set the **Pixel Offset** to {-420, -90}.

3. Duplicate the **Label** GameObject from **Nickname** and perform the following steps:

    1. Drag it inside the **Volume** GameObject.

    2. Drag our Volume's **Background** GameObject inside the **Container** field.

    3. Change its text to [AAFFFF]Volume.

4. Select the **Slider** GameObject.

5. Attach a component to it by navigating to **NGUI | Attach | Anchor** and perform the following steps:

    1. Drag the **Background** GameObject from **Volume** inside the **Container** field.

    2. Set **Pixel Offset** to {-100, -23}.

6. Select the **Background** GameObject from **Slider** and perform the following steps:

    1. Enter **Depth** as 3.

    2. In the **Color Tint** parameter, change **R** to 80, **G** to 220, **B** to 85, and **A** to 255.

7. Select the **Foreground** GameObject from **Slider** and perform the following steps:

    1. Enter **Depth** as 4.

    2. In the **Color Tint** parameter, change **R** to 95, **G** to 255, **B** to 190, and **A** to 255.

8. Select the **Thumb** GameObject from the **Slider** and perform the following steps:

    1. Enter **Depth** as 5.

    2. In the **Color Tint** parameter, change **R** to 100, **G** to 255, **B** to 250, and **A** to 255.

Ok, we now have a nice volume slider! Your **Hierarchy** view should look like the following screenshot:

We will now link it to the game's volume with a new script. Let's add some music to our main menu. First, add an audio file of your choice to your Unity project as shown in the following steps:

1. Select our **Main Camera** GameObject.

2. Attach a component to it by navigating to **Component | Audio | AudioSource** and perform the following steps:

    1. Drag a music file from the **Project** view to the **AudioSource** parameter's **Audio Clip** field.

3. Select the **Slider** GameObject from **Volume** and perform the following steps:

    1. Create and attach a new VolumeManager.cs C# script to it.

    2. Open this new VolumeManager.cs script.

In this new script, we will first need to declare and initialize the necessary variables. Add the following variable declarations and the Awake() method:

```
//We will need the Slider
UISlider slider;

void Awake ()
{
  //Get the Slider
  slider = GetComponent<UISlider>();
  //Set the Slider's value to last saved volume
  slider.value = NGUITools.soundVolume;
}
```

Here we initialized the slider's value to NGUITools.soundVolume because this float is persistent and will be saved across scenes—even if you exit the game.

Now let's create an OnVolumeChange() method that will modify our AudioListener method's volume each time the slider's value is changed:

```
public void OnVolumeChange ()
{
  //Change NGUI's UI Sounds volume
  NGUITools.soundVolume = UISlider.current.value;
  //Change the Game AudioListener's volume
  AudioListener.volume = UISlider.current.value;
}
```

Ok, the method is ready. We just need to call it each time the slider's value changes. Let's use the **UISlider** component's **Notify** field as follows:

1. Select the **Slider** GameObject from **Volume** and perform the following steps:

    1. Drag-and-drop the **Slider** GameObject from **Volume** into the **Notify** field.
    2. For the **Method** field, select VolumeManager.OnVolumeChange.

Now, each time the slider's value is modified, our method will be called.

You can hit the Play button; the game's volume will change with the slider. The volume is saved even when you exit the game and restart!

Toggle

Now that we have a volume slider, let's add an enable/disable sound checkbox, which will turn down the volume to 0 and hide our volume slider.

First, create a toggle widget as follows:

1. Select the **Panel** GameObject and create a new child with *Alt + Shift + N*.
2. Rename that new child as Sound. It will be our sound toggle container.
3. Navigate to **NGUI | Open | Widget Wizard** and perform the following steps:

    1. Select **Toggle** as **Template**.
    2. Select the **Dark** Sprite as **Background**.
    3. Select the **X** Sprite as **Checkmark**.
    4. With the **Sound** container selected, click on the **Add To** button.

A checkbox with a label has just been created as shown in the following screenshot:

Parameters

Select our new **Toggle** GameObject. Let's look at the UIToggle's **Inspector** parameters:

- **Group**: This is the toggle's group. Toggles of the same group will act as radio buttons; only one of them can be checked at once.
- **Start State**: This defines in which state the toggle will be at the start.
- **Animation**: This is the animation that will play when the checkbox changes state.
- **Sprite**: This lets us choose the widget to be used as a checkmark; we should use our **X** sprite here.
- **Transition**: This is either **Smooth** or **Instant**; uses alpha fade in / fade out.
- **Notify**: This is the GameObject to notify on when toggled. When a GameObject is assigned, you may choose a public method to call on a toggle event.

Creating a sound toggle

We have seen the UIToggle's parameters. Now we will create this sound toggle as shown in the following screenshot:

Let's use our recently added **Toggle** GameObject to create the window shown here. Follow these steps to do so:

1. Select both the **Background** and **Label** GameObjects from **Volume** and perform the following steps:
    1. Duplicate them.
    2. Drag-and-drop those new duplicates inside our **Sound** container.

2. Select the **Background** GameObject from **Sound** and enter its UIAnchor's **Pixel Offset** parameter as {-420, 43}.

3. Select the **Label** GameObject from **Sound** and change its text to [AAFFFF] Sound.

4. Select the **Toggle** GameObject and check the **Start State** Boolean in **UIToggle**.

5. Attach a component to it by navigating to **NGUI | Attach | Anchor** and perform the following steps:

   1. Drag the **Background** GameObject from **Sound** inside the **Container** field.

   2. Enter its **Pixel Offset** parameter as {-38, -20}.

6. Add a component to it by navigating to **NGUI | Interaction | Toggled Objects**, and drag our **Volume** container GameObject into the **Activate** array.

7. Select the **Background** sprite GameObject from **Toggle** and perform the following steps:

   1. Enter **Depth** as 3.

   2. In the **Color Tint** parameter, change **R** to 130, **G** to 255, **B** to 130, and **A** to 255.

8. Select the **Checkmark** sprite GameObject from **Toggle** and perform the following steps:

   1. Enter **Depth** as 4.

   2. In the **Color Tint** parameter, change **R** to 50, **G** to 255, **B** to 70, and **A** to 255.

9. Select the **Label** GameObject from **Toggle** and perform the following steps:

   1. Enter **Depth** as 3.

   2. Change its text to [AAFFFF] Enabled.

   3. In the **Color Tint** parameter, change **R** to 200, **G** to 255, **B** to 250, and **A** to 255.

Hit the Play button. We have a nice sound box with a sound toggle checkbox that hides/shows the **Volume** box when needed. But it does not turn off the sound yet.

We need to make some changes to our VolumeManager.cs script to correct this.

First, open our `VolumeManager.cs` script. We will add a new `OnSoundToggle()` method that will be called when the toggle changes state. It will set the volume directly to 0, or to the slider's value. Add this new method to `VolumeManager.cs` as shown in the following code lines:

```
public void OnSoundToggle()
{
    float newVolume = 0;
    //If sound toggled ON, set new volume to slider value
    if(UIToggle.current.value)
    newVolume = slider.value;
    //Apply newVolume to volumes
    AudioListener.volume = newVolume;
    NGUITools.soundVolume = newVolume;
}
```

Ok, the previous method will set both our volumes to 0 or the slider's value, depending on the toggle's state. Let's link it to our sound's toggle by selecting our **Toggle** GameObject and dragging the **Slider** GameObject from **Volume** inside the **Notify** field in **UIToggle**, below the **On Value Change** section. Then, for the **Method** field, select `VolumeManager.OnSoundToggle`.

Hit the Play button. That's it. When we click on the **Toggle** checkbox from **Volume**, the volume reacts accordingly.

But if we turn the sound off using the toggle and stop running, when we hit Play again, the checkbox is still checked and the volume slider is displayed, but the volume is at 0.

That's because our volume is set to 0, but the checkbox is still checked at start. Let's add a simple line of code that will set the start state to `false` if the volume is at 0:

1. Open our `VolumeManager.cs` script.

2. Declare a new global variable named `public UIToggle soundToggle`.

3. At the end of the `Awake()` method, add the following lines of code:

    ```
    //If volume is at 0, uncheck the Sound Checkbox
    if(NGUITools.soundVolume == 0) soundToggle.value = false;
    ```

4. Save the script and return to Unity.

5. Select the **Slider** GameObject from **Volume**.

Drag the**Toggle** GameObject from **Volume** in the volume manager's **Sound Toggle** field.

Hit the Play button. That's it. If you disable sound using the toggle and exit the Play mode and then launch it again, the checkbox stays unchecked and the volume slider is not displayed. Perfect!

Popup list

We will now learn how to create the popup list, see its parameters, and create a difficulty selector for our game.

1. Select the **Panel** GameObject and create a new child with *Alt + Shift + N*.

2. Rename that new child as `Difficulty`. It's our difficulty box container.

3. Navigate to **NGUI | Open | Widget Wizard** and perform the following steps:

   1. Select **Popup List** as **Template**

   2. Select **Dark** as **Foreground**.

   3. Select **Dark** as **Background**.

   4. Select the **Highlight** sprite as **Highlight**.

4. With our **Difficulty** GameObject selected, click on the **Add To** button.

Parameters

A **Popup List** GameObject has just been created. Let's look at its parameters:

- **Atlas**: This is the atlas used for the popup list's sprites.
- **Font**: This is the font used for the popup list's options.
- **Text Label**: This is the label to update when **Popup List** changes selection.
- **Options**: This is the list of options that will pop up — one per line.
- **Default**: This is the option selected at start.
- **Position**: You may force the list of options to appear `Above` or `Below` the Popup List's button. If this parameter is set to `Auto`, NGUI will choose one of both depending on the available space.
- **Localized**: This enables localization on options.
- **Background**: This is the background sprite for the popup list's options container.
- **Highlight**: This is the sprite for the currently hovered option.
- **Text Color**: This is the options list's text color tint.

- **Background**: This is the popup list's background color tint.
- **Highlight**: This is the hovered option's background color tint.
- **Padding**: This is the padding of the **X** and **Y** options.
- **Text Scale**: This is the options' text scale.
- **Animated**: If this is unchecked, the options' display will be instantaneous.
- **Notify**: This is the GameObject that lets you choose a method to call when the selected option changes.

Below the `UIPopup List` component, we have the usual `UIButton` and `UIPlay Sound` components that we have already seen before.

[A Popup Menu template is also available in the Widget Wizard. The only difference is that the menu does not indicate which choice you have selected; the button's label is not updated.]

Creating a difficulty selector

We will now use our new **Popup List** GameObject to select the game's difficulty level as shown in the following screenshot:

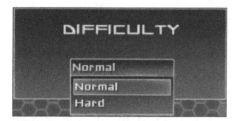

Let's create this difficulty selector as shown in the following steps:

1. Select the **Background** and **Label** GameObjects from **Sound** and perform the following steps:
   1. Duplicate them.
   2. Drag-and-drop them into our **Difficulty** container.

2. Select the **Background** GameObject from **Difficulty** and enter its **Pixel Offset** parameter to {420, 43}.

3. Select the **Label** GameObject from **Difficulty** and change its text to [AAFFFF] Difficulty.

4. Select our **Popup List** in the **Hierarchy** view and perform the following steps:

    1. Rename it as Popup.

    2. Type in Normal and Hard separated by a line.

    3. In **Text Color**, change **R** to 190, **G** to 250, **B** to 255, and **A** to 255.

    4. In **Background**, change **R** to 70, **G** to 250, **B** to 255, and **A** to 255.

    5. In **Highlight**, change **R** to 70, **G** to 255, **B** to 150, and **A** to 255.

    6. In **Hover**, change **R** to 70, **G** to 255, **B** to 150, and **A** to 255.

5. Attach a component to it by navigating to **NGUI | Attach | Anchor** and perform the following steps:

    1. Drag the **Background** GameObject from **Difficulty** in the **Container** field.

    2. Enter **Pixel Offset** as {-76, -20}.

6. Select our popup's **Sprite** GameObject and perform the following steps:

    1. In **Color Tint**, change **R** to 170, **G** to 255, **B** to 190, and **A** to 255.

    2. Enter **Depth** as 3.

7. Select our popup's **Label** GameObject and perform the following steps:

    1. In **Color Tint**, change **R** to 135, **G** to 255, **B** to 170, and **A** to 255.

    2. Enter **Depth** as 4.

Ok, we now have a **Popup List** GameObject that lets us select the game's difficulty level. Your **Hierarchy** panel should look like the following screenshot:

Now it's time to link it to a method that will take that difficulty into account. Do this by performing the following steps:

1. Open our `GameManager.cs` script.

2. Declare a new enum for our difficulty levels as follows:

    ```
    public enum Difficulties
    {
      Normal,
      Hard
    }
    ```

3. Declare a new `Difficulty` variable to store the current difficulty as follows:

    ```
    public static Difficulties Difficulty =
      Difficulties.Normal;
    ```

We used a static variable because it won't be destroyed when loading the game scene. By default, the difficulty level is set to **Normal**.

Now we need to add the `OnDifficultyChange()` method that will change our `Difficulty` variable when **Popup List** changes state as follows:

```
public void OnDifficultyChange()
{
  //If Difficulty changes to Normal, set Difficulties.Normal
  if(UIPopupList.current.value == "Normal")
  Difficulty = Difficulties.Normal;
  //Otherwise, set it to Hard
  else Difficulty = Difficulties.Hard;
}
```

Our method is ready; we need to call it when **Popup List** changes state. Do so by performing the following steps:

1. Save all the modified scripts and return to Unity.

2. Select the **Popup List** GameObjectfrom **Difficulty** and perform the following steps:

    1. Drag our **GameManager** GameObject into the **Notify** field.

    2. For the **Method** field, select `GameManager.OnDifficultyChange`.

Now, the **Popup List** GameObject will change the `Difficulty` variable according to its value. We will be able to access this static variable once we're in the game.

Summary

In this chapter, we have learned how to create and configure most of NGUI's widgets—sprites, labels, buttons, text inputs, sliders, toggles, and popup lists.

We now have a main menu with interactive elements. We also used NGUI's notification event system to change variables in code and register the user's choices.

We used **UIAnchors** and **UIStretch** components to properly position our widgets—we just have to move each box's background sprite to move the entire element. This is much more effective than having to move each GameObject manually! You should have a main menu that looks like the following screenshot:

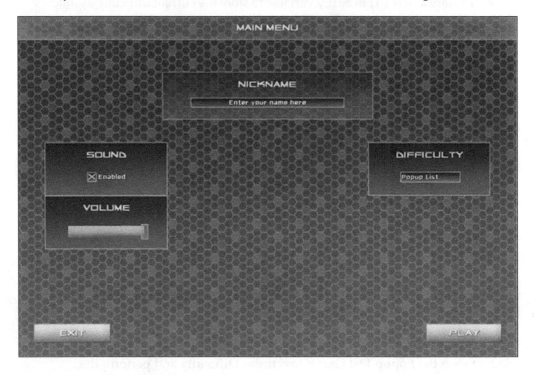

Ok, now it is time to enhance our UI experience and make this better. Let's move on to *Chapter 3*, *Enhancing your UI*.

3
Enhancing your UI

In this chapter, we will learn how to enhance our UI experience by using more advanced features, which are as follows:

- Draggable panels and animations
- The drag-and-drop system
- Automatic content alignment
- Clipping
- Scrollable text
- The localization system

Let's start by talking about NGUI components and their overall behavior.

NGUI components

In *Chapter 2, Creating Widgets*, we added the **UIStretch** and **UIAnchor** components to our widgets, and also the **Load Level On Click** component. There are many more components, and the purpose of this chapter is to discuss these components. We will use the most important ones in this chapter. It is possible to add a component to any kind of widget—considering it is logical of course.

This component-oriented structure makes NGUI extremely flexible and modular. We will start by making our main menu a draggable window.

The draggable panel

We will now learn how to turn our menu into a draggable window. Let's add the correct component to it and study its parameters, which are as follows:

1. Select the **Panel** GameObject.

2. Rename it as `MainMenu`.

3. Attach the **Draggable Panel** component to it by navigating to **Component | NGUI | Interaction**.

The **MainMenu** GameObject now has a **UIDraggable Panel** component attached to it.

Parameters

The following are the 13 parameters for setting values in the **UIDraggable Panel**:

- **Drag Effect**: This is the effect used while dragging the panel to have a smoother drag.

- **Restrict Within Panel**: This uses the parent panel to restrain the draggable panel within its clipping bounds.

- **Disable Drag If Fits**: If the content fits the parent panel's clipping bounds, dragging will be disabled.

- **Smooth Drag Start**: This avoids a "jump" effect on drag start.

- **Reposition Clipping**: This repositions the **Clipping** to the **Top Left Corner** immediately.

- **IOS Drag Emulation**: Dragging movement speed is reduced when overpassing the clipping edges.

- **Scroll Wheel Factor**: If you want the scroll wheel to drag the panel on the y axis, set this value to greater than 0.

- **Momentum Amount**: This is the effect applied when the panel is dropped. The panel will keep moving after releasing the scroll wheel.

- **Horizontal Scroll Bar**: This lets you drag a scroll bar to define it as the panel's horizontal scroll bar.

- **Vertical Scroll Bar**: This lets you drag another scroll bar to define it as the panel's vertical scroll bar.

- **Show Scroll Bars**: This allows you to show scroll bars always, show them only if necessary, or show them while dragging.

- **Scale**: This defines which axis the panel should drag on: 0 means no dragging, 1 allows full dragging on this axis.

- **Relative Position On Reset**: This is the offset relative to the mouse's position. It is useful if you want an offset from the mouse's position while dragging.

Now that we have seen the component's parameters, let's use them to drag our main menu.

Dragging the MainMenu

We have added the **UIDraggable Panel** component that sets this **UIPanel** as a **Draggable Panel**. Now, we must mark our **MainMenu** as the GameObject that holds the draggable content.

We will also add a **Box Collider** component to define where the user must click to drag the panel:

1. Select our **MainMenu** GameObject and perform the following steps:
   1. Set the **Clipping** parameter of **UIPanel** to **Alpha Clip**.
   2. Set the **Size** field in **Clipping** to 1920 x 1080.
   3. Uncheck the **IOS Drag Emulation** Boolean.

2. Add the **Drag Panel Contents** component to it.

3. Add the **Box Collider** component to it and perform the following steps:
   1. Check the **Is Trigger** Boolean — we don't need collisions, just a trigger to receive Raycasts from the **UICamera**.
   2. Set its **Center** coordinates to {0, 395, 0}.
   3. Set its **Size** coordinates to {1300, 62, 1}.

Click on the play button. By clicking on the window's title, you can drag the main menu. But still, it isn't configured correctly; you can only move it on the x axis.

Let's change an important parameter of the **UIDraggable Panel** component of **MainMenu** to allow dragging on the x axis by performing the following steps:

1. Select our **MainMenu** GameObject.

2. Set **Scale** in **UIDraggable Panel** to {1, 1, 0}.

And that's it! Our **MainMenu** is now draggable on both the axes. If you drag it outside the screen, it will move back inside when dropped. We had to define a clipping of the screen's size for this **Restrict Within Panel** function to work.

The drag-and-drop system

We will now create our own **drag-and-drop** system that will enable the user to select a power. They will be able to drag one of the two available powers inside a selection box as shown in the following screenshot:

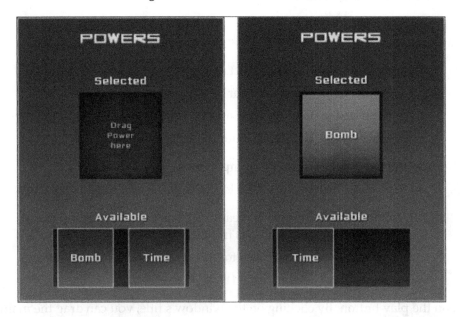

Powers selection

Let's create a drag-and-drop system to select which of the two powers the player can choose: a **Bomb** power, which will explode or a **Time** power, which will slow down time for a few seconds.

Draggable items container

Let's start by creating a nice box for our powers and a draggable items container by performing the following steps:

1. Select our **MainMenu** GameObject and perform the given steps:
    1. Create a new empty child GameObject by pressing *Alt + Shift + N.*
    2. Rename it as `Powers`.

2. Select the **Background** and **Label** GameObjects from **Sound**:
    1. Duplicate them.
    2. Drag these new duplicates inside our **Powers** GameObject.

3. Select the **Background** GameObject in **Powers** and perform these steps:
    1. Set its **Dimensions** to `320 x 420`.
    2. Set the **Pixel Offset** in **UIAnchor** to {`0, -100`}.

4. Select the **Label** GameObject in **Powers**:
    1. Rename it as `TitleLabel`.
    2. Change its text to `[AAFFFF] Powers`.

5. Select the **Label** GameObject, which is a child of **Title**, and perform the following steps:
    1. Duplicate it.
    2. Rename this new duplicate as `SelectedLabel`.
    3. Drag it inside our **Powers** GameObject.
    4. Drag our **Background** GameObject in **Powers** to the **Container** field in its **UIAnchor**.
    5. Set its **Side** parameter in **UIAnchor** to **Top**.
    6. Set its **Pixel Offset** in **UIAnchor** to {`0, -95`}.
    7. Change its **Font** to `SciFi Font - Normal`.
    8. Change its text to `[AAFFFF] Selected`.

6. Select our **SelectedLabel** GameObject in **Powers** and perform the following steps:
    1. Duplicate it.
    2. Rename this new duplicate as `AvailableLabel`.
    3. Change its text to `[AAFFFF] Available`.
    4. Set its **Pixel Offset** in **UIAnchor** to {`0, -295`}.

7. Select our **SelectedLabel GameObject** in **Powers** and perform these steps:

    1. Duplicate it.
    2. Rename this new duplicate it as `InstructionsLabel`.
    3. Change text to `[55AA99]Drag Power Here`—one word per line.
    4. Set its **Overflow** parameter to **Shrink Content**.
    5. Set its **Depth** to 4.
    6. Set its **Dimensions** to `128 x 45`.
    7. Set its **Pixel Offset** in **UIAnchor** to {0, -175}.

8. Select our **Background** sprite GameObject in **Powers** and perform the following steps:

    1. Duplicate it.
    2. Rename this new duplicate as `PowersContainer`.
    3. Set its **Dimensions** to `215 x 90`.
    4. Set its **Color Tint** to {100, 100, 100, 255}.
    5. Set its **Depth** to 3.
    6. Drag our **AvailableLabel** GameObject from **Powers** to the **Container** field in its **UIAnchor**.
    7. Set its **Pixel Offset** in **UIAnchor** to {0, -60}.

Ok, we now have our powers box with the correct labels and a background.

Draggable items

Now that we have the PowersContainer, let's create the following two draggable items:

Follow the ensuing steps to create them:

1. Select our **PowersContainer** GameObject in **Powers**.

2. Create a new child GameObject with *Alt + Shift + N* and rename it as Bomb.

3. Attach a **Collider** object to it by navigating to **NGUI | Attach**. It will be used to detect the mouse and receive the correct messages for the drag-and-drop system by performing the following steps:

    1. Check the **Is Trigger** Boolean.

    2. Set its **Size** field of new **Box Collider** to {90, 90, 1}.

4. Attach a **Drag Object** component to it by navigating to **Component | NGUI | Interaction**:

    1. Drag our **Bomb** from **PowersContainer** in its **Target** field.

    2. Set its **Scale** to {1, 1, 0}.

    3. Set the **Momentum Amount** to 0.

5. Select and duplicate the **Background** sprite GameObject in **Powers**. Then perform the following steps:

    1. Drag it inside our new **Bomb** GameObject.

    2. Set its **Depth** to 5.

    3. Set its **Dimensions** to 90 x 90.

    4. Remove its **UIAnchor** component.

    5. Reset its **Transform** position values to {0, 0, 0}.

6. Select and duplicate the **AvailableLabel** GameObject in **Powers**. Then perform these steps:

    1. Rename that new duplicate as Label.

    2. Drag it inside our new **Bomb** GameObject.

    3. Change its text to [AAFFFF] Bomb.

    4. Set its **Depth** to 6.

    5. Remove its **UIAnchor** component.

    6. Reset its **Transform** position values to {0, 0, 0}.

7. Select our **Bomb** GameObject.

8. Attach a **Button Color** component to it by navigating to **Component | NGUI | Interaction** and perform these steps:

    1. Drag our **Background** GameObject from **Bomb** to the **Target** field.

    2. Set its **Pressed** color to {0, 255, 0, 150}.

9. Create a new `DragItem.cs` C# script and attach this script to the **Button Color** component.

We have one draggable Bomb power with a `DragItem.cs` script attached to it. Let's create the second Time power by performing the following steps:

1. Select and duplicate our **Bomb** GameObject in **PowersContainer**.

2. Rename that new duplicate as `Time`.

3. Select our new **Label** GameObject, which is a child of **Time**.

4. Change its text to `[AAFFFF]Time`.

Ok, we now have our two draggable Powers, and they are on top of each other. Let's correct this using Anchors and a Grid component, which will automatically align our items. We can do this using the following steps:

1. Select our **PowersContainer** GameObject.

2. Create a new child by pressing *Alt + Shift + N* and rename this new child as `Grid`.

3. Attach a **Grid** component to it by navigating to **Component | NGUI | Interaction**.

4. Drag both our **Bomb** and **Time** GameObjects in our new **Grid** GameObject.

5. Select our **Grid** GameObject and perform the following steps:

    1. Set its **Cell Width** to `105`.

    2. Check the **Sorted** Boolean.

    3. Check the **Reposition Now** Boolean to update the table.

    4. Set its **Transform** position to {-52, 0, 0}.

The UIGrid component automatically aligns its children. We now have our two draggable powers aligned. If you click on play, you'll see that you can drag them around as shown in the following screenshot:

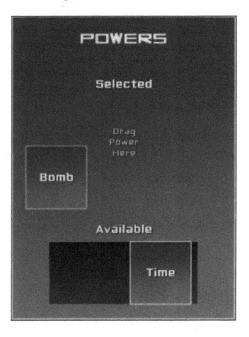

The drop surface

We will create a new **Surface** GameObject with a `DropSurface.cs` script and a **Box Collider** component to define where the draggable items can be dropped.

When the user drops an object with a **DragItem** component on the **Surface** GameObject, the **DragItem** component will be destroyed, and a "dropped version" of the object will be instantiated as a child of the **Surface** GameObject.

First, let's create and configure the **Surface** GameObject by performing the following steps:

1. Select and duplicate our **Background** GameObject from **Powers** and rename this new duplicate as `Surface`.

2. Select our new **Surface** GameObject from **Powers** and perform these steps:

   1. Change its **Sprite** to **Highlight**.

   2. Change its **Color Tint** to {0, 25, 5, 255}.

   3. Set its **Depth** to 3.

   4. Set its **Dimensions** to 130 x 130.

   5. Drag our **SelectedLabel** GameObject from **Powers** to the **Container** field in its **UIAnchor**.

   6. Set its **Pixel Offset** to {0, -80}.

3. Attach a **Collider** object to it by navigating to **NGUI | Attach | Collider**. It will detect **DragItems**. Then perform the following steps:

   1. Check its **Is Trigger** Boolean.

   2. Set its **Size** to {130, 130, 1}.

4. Create and attach a new `DropSurface.cs` C# script to it.

Good, our surface is now ready to detect our items.

Prefab instantiated on drop

Now, we need to create two prefabs for our powers that will be instantiated as children of the **Surface** GameObject when a **DragItem** component is dropped on it. They will look as follows:

Let's create these prefabs by performing the following steps:

1. Select the **Bomb** GameObject from **Grid** and the following steps:

   1. Duplicate it.

   2. Rename it as `SelectedBomb`.

2. Select our new **SelectedBomb** GameObject from **Grid**. Then perform the following steps:

   1. Change its **Normal** color tint to **R**: 0, **G**: 145, **B**: 60, and **A**: 255.

   2. Remove its **Box Collider** component.

   3. Remove its **Drag Item** component.

3. Create and attach a new `Power.cs` C# script to it.

4. Select the **Background** sprite GameObject from **SelectedBomb**. Then perform the following steps:

   1. Change the **Sprite** to **Light**.

   2. Set its **Depth** to 4.

   3. Set its **Dimensions** to 120 x 120.

5. Select the **Label** GameObject from **SelectedBomb** and set its **Depth** to 5.

6. Drag our **SelectedBomb** GameObject into a folder of your choice in your **Project** view to create a prefab from it.

7. Once our **SelectedBomb** is a prefab (blue in the scene's **Hierarchy**), you may delete it from the scene.

We now have our **SelectedBomb** prefab. Let's declare a variable in our `DragItem.cs` script that will store the prefab to instantiate on drop. We can do this by following the ensuing steps:

1. Select our **Bomb** GameObject from **Grid**.

2. Open the `DragItem.cs` script attached to it and add this public variable using the following code:

   ```
   public Object CreateOnDrop;
   ```

3. Save the script and go back to Unity.

4. Select our **Bomb** GameObject from **Grid** and drag our **SelectedBomb** prefab from the Project view in the **Create On Drop** field in its **Drag Item**.

Now let's do the same for our **Time** power in the following manner:

1. Select our **SelectedBomb** prefab in the **Project** view and perform the following steps:

   1. Duplicate it with *Ctrl* + *D*.

   2. Rename the new duplicate prefab as `SelectedTime`.

2. Select its **Label** child GameObject and change its text to [AAFFFF] Time.

3. Select our **Time** GameObject from **Grid** in the scene's **Hierarchy**.

4. Drag our **SelectedTime** prefab from the **Project** view in the **Create On Drop** field in its **Drag Item**.

We can now add an OnDrop() method to our DropSurface.cs script to handle dropped objects in the following manner:

1. Select our **Surface** GameObject from **Powers**.

2. Open its attached DropSurface.cs script.

The OnDrop() event has one argument: the dropped GameObject. Let's add this method to our script to handle the drop by using the following code snippet:

```
//Called when an object is dropped on DropSurface
public void OnDrop(GameObject dropped)
{
  //Get the DragItem from the dropped object
  DragItem dragItem = dropped.GetComponent<DragItem>();
  //If it has none, don't go further
  if(dragItem == null) return;
  //Instantiate the defined CreateOnDrop Object
  GameObject newPower = NGUITools.AddChild(this.gameObject,
  dragItem.CreateOnDrop as GameObject);
  //Destroy the dropped Object
  Destroy(dropped);
}
```

Save the script and click on the play button. When you drop a power on the **Surface** GameObject, nothing happens! Why?

That's because the OnDrop() event depends on the Raycast from Camera, and at the moment of the drop, our dragged power's **Box Collider** component is in the way of the mouse cursor and the **Surface** GameObject.

We just have to disable the collider of **Power** while it is dragged. We can do this in the following manner:

1. Select our **Bomb** GameObject from **Grid**.

2. Open its attached DragItem.cs script.

We will use the OnPress() event to do this. The OnPress() method will take the object's pressed state as an argument in the following manner:

```
//Method called when the Item is Pressed or Released
void OnPress(bool pressed)
{
  //Invert the collider's state
  collider.enabled = !pressed;
}
```

Save the script and click on play. You can now drag-and-drop the powers on the surface!

Handling an invalid drop

Now, let's make sure power is repositioned to its default position if the user drops it outside the **Surface** GameObject.

To achieve this, we can check the camera's last hit when the OnPress(false) event occurs. Open our DragItem.cs and add the following lines after collider.enabled = !pressed:

```
//If the Item is released
if(!pressed)
{
  //Get the last hit collider
  Collider col = UICamera.lastHit.collider;
  //If there is no collider, or no DropSurface behind the Power
  if(col == null || col.GetComponent<DropSurface>() == null)
  {
    //Get the grid in parent objects
    UIGrid grid = NGUITools.FindInParents<UIGrid>(gameObject);
    //If a grid is found, order it to Reposition now
    if(grid != null) grid.Reposition();
  }
}
```

Save and click on play. If you drop a Power anywhere but on the **Surface** GameObject, our items will be repositioned automatically. Great!

A slight problem: you can drop both of them on the surface, and then you're stuck. Let's explore the solution in the following sections.

Replacing the current item

We will now ensure that you can only have one power on the surface. If you drag a second one while the DropSurface is already occupied, the current power will be replaced by the new one and the drag item component will reappear in the **PowersContainer** GameObject.

We will need to know which power is currently dropped on the surface and which original drag Item component must be instantiated in **Grid** in **PowersContainer**:

1. Select our **SelectedBomb** prefab in the **Project** view.

2. Open its attached `Power.cs` script.

This script will be used to contain information about the dropped item. Let's declare a new `enum` to distinguish which type of power, and an `Object` variable to set which prefab will be instantiated to make the draggable item in power reappear when replaced:

```
//Declare an enum to define type of Power
public enum Type
{
  None,
  Time,
  Bomb
}
//Declare a Type variable to choose it in Inspector
public Type type;
//Object variable to define the DragItem to recreate
public Object createOnDestroy;
```

Now, we need to go back to Unity and create prefabs for our `Bomb` and `Time` draggable items before we assign them to the `createOnDestroy` variables:

1. Select our **Bomb** GameObject from **Powers** in the **Hierarchy** of **Scene** and drag it into a folder of your choice in your **Project** view to create a prefab from it.

2. Select our **SelectedBomb** Prefab in the **Project** view and perform the following steps:

    1. Set its **Power** component's **Type** variable to **Bomb**.

    2. Drag our new **Bomb** Prefab from the Project view to the **Power** component's **Create On Destroy** field.

We assigned the **Type** parameter of **SelectedBomb** to **Bomb**, and it now has an assigned prefab that we will instantiate to recreate the draggable item when it gets replaced.

 Repeat steps 1 and 2, replacing the word Bomb with Time to do the same for our Time power GameObject and prefab.

Now, we have to code a system that will register which type of power is currently selected. We'll use the GameManager.cs script in the following manner to store it:

1. Open our GameManager.cs script and declare this new static variable:

   ```
   //This static variable will contain the selected power
   public static Power.Type SelectedPower = Power.Type.None;
   ```

2. Add this new static method to set our SelectedPower from other scripts:

   ```
   //This static method changes the SelectedPower value
   public static void SetPower(Power.Type newPower)
   {
      SelectedPower = newPower;
   }
   ```

Ok, we now have a method to register the currently selected power. It is time to modify our DropSurface.cs script:

1. Select our **Surface** GameObject from **Powers** and open the DropSurface.cs script.

2. Declare a new GameObject variable to store our **Grid** GameObject:

   ```
   public GameObject dragItemsContainer;
   ```

3. Save the script, select our **Surface** GameObject from **Powers** in the **Hierarchy** view. Drag our **Grid** GameObject from **PowersContainer** in its **DropSurface** component's **Drag Items Container** field.

Now, go back to our DropSurface.cs script. We will add these following lines to handle the fact that the user cannot drop two powers on the surface; it will replace the previous one and recreate its original Drag Item. In the OnDrop() method, just below the if(dragItem == null) return line, add the following:

```
RecreateDragItem();
```

Now, add a new `RecreateDragItem()` method to the file:

```
void RecreateDragItem()
{
  //If there's already a Power selected
  if(GameManager.SelectedPower != Power.Type.None)
  {
    //Get the selected power's Power.cs script
    Power selectedPowerScript =
      transform.GetChild(0).GetComponent<Power>();
    //Add the Drag Item to the grid
    NGUITools.AddChild(dragItemsContainer,
      selectedPowerScript.createOnDestroy as GameObject);
    //Destroy the currently selected Power
    Destroy(selectedPowerScript.gameObject);
  }
}
```

Ok, we now have to inform the `GameManager.cs` script that the selected Power has changed. We can do this by calling our `SetPower()` static method.

Add the following line in the `OnDrop()` method just before the `Destroy (dropped)` line:

```
//Set the new selected power in the GameManager
GameManager.SetPower(newPower.GetComponent<Power>().type);
```

Save all the scripts and click on the play button. You can drop the first Power on the **Surface** GameObject and then drop the second one. The first power is now replaced and will reappear in the **Available** power container.

Unfortunately, we cannot simply remove the power. Let's correct this in the following sections.

Removing the current item

We want to remove the selected power by clicking on it. In our `DropSurface.cs` script, add this new `OnClick()` method that will be called when the user clicks on the surface:

```
void OnClick()
{
  //Recreate the DragItem now
  RecreateDragItem();
  //Reset SelectedPower to None
```

```
GameManager.SetPower(Power.Type.None);
//Force reposition of the grid
dragItemsContainer.GetComponent<UIGrid>().Reposition();
}
```

Now click on play. You can now remove the selected power by right- or left-clicking on it.

Animations with NGUI

One great aspect of NGUI is that you can use Unity's animation system on any kind of widget. There also are some Tween components that let you modify most values over time, such as dimensions, color, and scale. For example, you can change an object's color from color A to color B in 5 seconds.

We have a nice main menu. But we actually have our options that are constantly displayed. That is not very user friendly.

We will use animations and tweens to hide our options and show them only when the user clicks on the **Options** button. With options hidden, our menu will look as shown in the following screenshot:

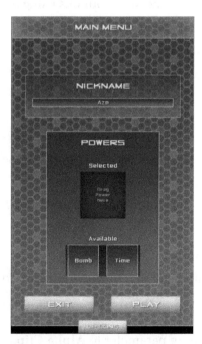

But first, let's make our powers' apparition smoother.

Smooth powers apparition

Let's add **Scale Tweens** on our prefabs to make them appear smoothly by performing the following steps:

1. In the Project view, select our **SelectedBomb** prefab.

2. Attach a **Scale Tween** component by navigating to **Component | NGUI | Tween** and perform the following steps:

    1. Set its **From** parameter to {0, 0, 0,}.

    2. Set its **Duration** to 0.2.

3. Right-click on the **Tween Scale** component and then click on **Copy Component**.

4. Select our **SelectedTime**, **Bomb**, and **Time** prefabs.

5. In the **Inspector** view, right-click on any existing component name and click on **Paste Component As New**.

Now, as soon as these widgets are created, they scale from 0 to 1 in 0.2 seconds, which makes them appear smoothly.

We can now see how we'll hide and show options using a button.

Clipping to hide options

First, we have to hide our option boxes. To do that, we will use **Panel Clipping** and increase their width when we need to show them. Let's set up the Clipping option:

1. Select our **Window** GameObject from **MainMenu** and set its **Dimensions** to 515 x 850.

2. Select the **MainMenu** GameObject and perform the following steps:

    1. Set its **Depth** in UIPanel to -1.

    2. Create a new child for **MainMenu** with *Alt* + *Shift* + *N*.

    3. Rename this new child as Container.

3. Select our new **Container** GameObject.

4. Attach a **Panel** component to it by navigating to **Component | NGUI | UI**. Then perform the following steps:

    1. Set its **Depth** to 0.

    2. Set its **Clipping** parameter to **Alpha Clip**.

    3. Set its **Size** to 515 x 1080.

5. Fold all the children of **MainMenu** using the arrow next to each of them.

6. Select every child of **MainMenu**, except the new **Container** child, and drag them all inside our new **Container** GameObject.

Good, our options are now hidden. Your **Hierarchy** should look as shown in the following screenshot:

Let's add an **Options** button that will show or hide these options:

1. Select and duplicate our **Play** GameObject from **Buttons** and rename this new duplicate as Options.

2. Select our new **Options** GameObject from **Buttons** and perform the following steps:

    1. Set its **Side** parameter in **UIAnchor** to **Bottom**.

    2. Reset its **Pixel Offset** in **UIAnchor** to {0, 0}.

    3. Set its **Size** in **Box Collider** to {140, 40, 0}.

    4. Remove its **Load Level On Click** component.

3. Select our **Background** GameObject from **Options** and set its **Dimensions** to 140 x 40.

4. Select our **Label** GameObject from **Options**:

    1. Change its text to Options.

    2. Set its **Overflow** parameter to **Shrink Content**.

    3. Set its **Dimensions** to 90 x 25.

Ok, so now we have an **Options** button. Next, we want it to enlarge our **Window** and the Panel Clipping width of **Container** when clicked. We can do this using code, but we will use tweens and animations in the following manner to see how they work:

1. Select our **Window** GameObject in **Container**.

2. Attach a **Tween Width** component to it by navigating to **Component | NGUI | Tween**. Then perform the following steps:

    1. Set its **From** parameter to 515.
    2. Set its **To** parameter to 1300.
    3. Set **Duration** to 0.5.
    4. Reset **Dimensions** to 515 x 850.
    5. Disable the **Tween Width** component to prevent it from tweening at start.

We have a **Tween** component that will resize the width of **Window** when activated. Let's use the **UIPlay Tween** component to start it when the **Options** button is clicked on:

1. Select our **Options** button GameObject.

2. Attach a **Play Tween** component by navigating to **Component | NGUI | Interaction**. Then perform the following steps:

    1. Drag our **Window** GameObject from **Container** in the **Tween Target** field.
    2. Set the **Play** direction to **Toggle**.

Click on play. You will see that the window resizes as needed when **Options** is clicked. However, the **Clipping** parameter doesn't. Let's correct this using a Unity animation:

1. Select our **Container** GameObject from **MainMenu**.
2. Open the **Animation** window by navigating to **Window | Animation**.
3. Click the red record button.
4. Save the animation as ShowOptions.anim and perform the following steps:

    1. Re-enter 515 for the clipping **X Size** from **UIPanel** to add a key.
    2. Move the time cursor in the **Animation** window to 0:30.
    3. Enter 1300 for the clipping **X Size** from **UIPanel** to add a key.
    4. Click on the red record button again to finish.

5. Uncheck its **Play Automatically** Boolean in the **Animation** component.

We have our animation ready. Now, let's link the button to the animation in the following manner:

1. Select our **Options** GameObject from **Buttons**.

2. Attach a Play Animation component to it by navigating to **Component | NGUI | Interaction**. Then perform the following steps:

    1. Drag our **Container** GameObject from **MainMenu** in the **Target** field.

    2. For the **Clip Name** parameter, type in ShowOptions.

    3. Set the **Play** direction to **Toggle**.

Click on play. Our window and clipping both resize perfectly in both directions when the **Options** button is clicked.

But you can see that our **Options** widgets aren't visible until you actually drag the main menu around; that's because the clipping is not refreshed after the animation.

1. To solve this, we can simply force a **Drag at the end of the Animation** option.

2. Select our **MainMenu** GameObject and perform the following steps:

    1. Create and add a new UpdatePanel.cs script to it.

    2. Open our new UpdatePanel.cs script.

3. Now, add this new UpdateNow() method to the script that will force a drag of $(0, 0, 0)$ value on our **MainMenu**:

```
public void UpdateNow()
{
  //Force a drag of {0, 0, 0} to update Panel
  GetComponent<UIDraggablePanel>().MoveRelative(Vector3.zero);
}
```

4. Save the script and then perform the following steps:

    1. Select our **Options** GameObject in **Buttons**.

    2. Drag our **MainMenu** GameObject in the **Notify** field of the **UIPlay Animation** component.

    3. Choose our new UpdatePanel.UpdateNow method for the **Method** field.

5. Click on the play button. The **Options** boxes now appear after the animation!

Great! We have used NGUI's **Tween** and **Play Animations** components to enhance our UI and make it nicer and more user friendly.

Scrollable text

Let's add a welcome textbox with instructions for the user. This text will be scrollable using the mouse wheel or a simple click-and-drag. It will look as shown in the following screenshot:

At the start, it will scroll automatically. Let's create it now:

1. Select our **Nickname** container GameObject, duplicate it by pressing *Ctrl + D*.

2. Rename this new duplicate as `Help`.

3. Select this **Help** GameObject and perform the following steps:

    1. Drag our **Title** GameObject in the **Container** field in its **UIAnchor**.

    2. Set its **Side** parameter in **UIAnchor** to **Bottom**.

    3. Set its **Pixel Offset** in **UIAnchor** to {0, -50}.

4. Attach a Panel component by navigating to **Component | NGUI | UI**:

    1. Set its **Depth** to 1.

    2. Set its **Clipping** parameter to **Alpha Clip**.

    3. Set its **Clipping Size** to 440 x 85.

5. Attach a **Collider** object to it by navigating to **NGUI | Attach** and set its **Size** to {440, 85, 0}.

6. Delete the **Input** GameObject from **Help**.

7. Select our **Label** GameObject from **Help** and perform the following steps:

    1. Change its **Font** to **SciFi Font – Normal**.

    2. Remove its **UIAnchor** component.

    3. Set its text to:

```
Welcome!
[HIT RETURN KEY]
[HIT RETURN KEY]
You can Select one of two [AAFFFF]Powers[FFFFFF]:
[AAFFAA]Bomb[FFFFFF]: Explodes all enemies at once
[AAFFAA]Time[FFFFFF]: Reduces Time speed for 10 seconds
```

8. Attach a **Tween Position** component to it by navigating to **Component | NGUI | Interaction**. Then perform the following steps:

    1. Set its **From** parameter to {0, -50, 0}.

    2. Set its **To** parameter to {0, 20, 0}.

    3. Set its **Duration** value to 1.5.

    4. Set its **Start Delay** value to 3.

9. Set its **Transform** position to {0, -50, 0}.

10. Select the **Background** GameObject from **Help** and perform the following steps:

    1. Set its **Dimensions** to 440 x 85.

    2. Set its **Color Tint** to {150, 255, 255, 255}.

Click on the play button. We now have a welcome text that scrolls automatically by changing its Y coordinate inside a clipped Panel. Let's enable the scroll wheel and mouse drag on this scrollable text:

1. Select our **Help** GameObject.

2. Attach a **Drag Object** component to it by navigating to **Component | NGUI | Interaction**. Then perform the following steps:

    1. Drag our **Label** GameObject from **Help** to the **Target** field.

    2. Set the **Scale** to {0, 1, 0} to limit to vertical scrolling.

    3. Set the **Scroll Wheel Factor** value to 1.

    4. Check the **Restrict Within Panel** Boolean.

Click on play. You can now drag the text label manually with either a left-click and drag or the mouse wheel. The **Box Collider** component on the **Help** GameObject detects mouse events, and the **UIDrag Object** reacts accordingly by changing the Y position of our **Label**.

We had to add a **UIPanel** component to the **Help** GameObject in order to restrict movement within the clipping's bounds.

Localization system

Now that we have a complete UI, let's configure the **localization system** and add a pop-up list to change our UI's language.

Localization files

All our localized text strings must be contained in a .txt file for each language. For the purpose of this book, we will have English and French, and we will need the English.txt file and the French.txt file.

Let's create them right now in the following manner:

1. Access your project's Assets folder with your file explorer and create a new folder named Localization.

2. Inside this new folder, create a new text document named English.txt.

3. Duplicate this new English.txt file and rename it as French.txt.

4. Open them both in your favorite IDE or text editor.

Ok, now our localization files are ready to be used with the localization system.

Localization component

We can now configure the localization system to work with our UI. We need to have the localization component attached to a GameObject in the scene:

1. Select our **GameManager** GameObject and attach a **Localization** component to it by navigating to **Component | NGUI | Internal**.

2. In the **Project** view, navigate to Assets | Localization and drag our English. txt and French.txt files in the languages array.

The **Starting Language** is set to **English**, and we also have **French** available in the array.

Language selection box

The next step is to create a **language selection box** as shown in the following screenshot:

If we want to see what we're doing, we should first disable the Clipping of our **Container** by setting the **Clipping** parameter in its **UIPanel** to **None**.

Once the Clipping is disabled, follow these steps:

1. Select the **Popup** GameObject from **Difficulty**:
    1. Check its **Localized** Boolean in **UIPopup List**.
    2. Rename its child **Label** GameObject as `CurrentDifficulty`.

2. Select and duplicate our **Difficulty** GameObject in **Container**.

3. Rename the new duplicate as `Language`.

4. Select our new **Background** GameObject in **Language** and set its **Pixel Offset** in **UIAnchor** to {`420, -90`}.

 Sometimes, anchors don't update themselves. You may need to deactivate and then activate the **Language** GameObject for the Label's **UIAnchor** to update.

5. Select our **Label** GameObject from **Language** and change its text to `[AAFFFF]Language`.

6. Select our **Popup** GameObject from `Language` and perform the following steps:
    1. Change the **Options** text value to have the following two options:
       ```
       English
       French
       ```
    2. Set its **Position** to **Below**.
    3. Check the **Localized** Boolean.

7. Attach a **Language Selection** component by navigating to **Component | NGUI | Interaction**.

8. Rename the **Label**, which is a child of **Popup**, as `CurrentLanguage`.

We can now reactivate **Clipping** in **Container** by setting the **Clipping** parameter in its **UIPanel** to **Alpha Clip**. The clipping **Size** has been saved.

That's it, our localization system is in place, and when the pop-up list changes value, the `Language Selection.cs` script automatically changes the localization's **Current Language** value.

Localizing a Label

We are now ready to localize our first Label using the **UILocalize** component and a Key that will define which string to use from our .txt files. Perform the following steps:

1. Select our **Label** GameObject from **Title**.

2. Attach a **Localize** component to it by navigating to **Component | NGUI | UI**.

3. Set its Key parameter by typing MainMenu.

4. Switch to our English.txt localization file and add the following line:

   ```
   MainMenu = [AAFFFF]Main Menu
   ```

5. Switch to our French.txt localization file and add the following line:

   ```
   MainMenu = [AAFFFF]Menu Principal
   ```

Save both the .txt files and click on the play button. If you access options and change the language to **French**, our window's title changes from **Main Menu** to **Menu Principal**. That's because the **UILocalize** component updates the **UILabel** component it's attached to using the string present after the = in our .txt localization file. If you exit the play mode, the language will be saved and the UI will be initialized with the last selected language.

Now, we must add a **UILocalize** component with its specific Key to every **Label** in the scene, then add a localization string for each of them in both of our .txt files.

Don't be afraid; it isn't that long, and it will train you to use the Localization System:

1. In the **Hierarchy** view, type Label inside the search box.

2. Select all the **Label** GameObjects matching the search by pressing *Ctrl + A* and attach a **Localize** component to the selection by navigating to **Component | NGUI | UI**.

3. Select our **Label** GameObject from **Title** and remove its second **UILocalize** component as it already had one!

Now, all of our **Label** GameObjects have a **UILocalize** component attached to them. One by one, select them and set their Key parameter based on their text set in the **UILabel** component.

You must ignore the Labels of **Popup List**; they don't need a **UILocalize** component since we checked their **Localized** Booleans. Simply add localization strings for their **Options** with the same names: **Normal**, **Hard**, **English**, and **French**.

Don't forget to apply the same operations to labels included in our four different powers prefabs: **Time**, **Bomb**, **SelectedTime**, and **SelectedBomb**. New lines (return) are replaced by \n in the localization files. Colors work identically.

When you're done with setting their Key parameters, switch to our English.txt file and add every key you need, plus = followed by the corresponding localized text.

Now, copy all of these keys declarations and paste them in our French.txt file and then replace the English words with French words or any other language you choose.

By the time you're finished, our entire UI will be localized!

Summary

In this chapter, we first learned how to set up a draggable panel. Then, we created and configured a drag-and-drop system to select which power we want using the **UIDrag Object** component and the custom code.

Remember to use the **UIGrid** component often to automatically align objects—they are very powerful when used wisely with **UIAnchor** and **UIStretch** components.

Using Unity's animations and NGUI's Tweens are no longer a secret for us—we used them to create a smooth apparition for these powers, and we combined them with Clipping to hide/show our Options menu.

Finally, we created scrollable text and learned how to use the Localization System to set up multiple languages.

We can now take a look at using C# with NGUI in the next chapter and see what we can accomplish using code.

4

C# with NGUI

In this chapter, we will talk about C# scripting with NGUI. We will learn how to handle events and interact with them. We'll use them to:

- Play animations and Tweens
- Change labels using localized text through code
- Add keyboard keys for our UI
- Create notifications and tool tips

We will also see some of the NGUI's code-oriented components, such as event forwarding and message sending.

Events methods

When using C# with NGUI, there are some methods that you will regularly use when you need to know if your object is currently hovered upon, pressed, or clicked.

If you attach a script to any object with a collider on it (for example, a button or a 3D object), you can add the following useful methods in the script to catch events:

- `OnHover(bool state)`: This method is called when the object is hovered or unhovered. The `state` bool gives the hover state; if `state` is `true`, the cursor just entered the object's collider. If `state` is `false`, the cursor has just left the collider's bounds.

- `OnPress(bool state)`: This method works in the exact same way as the previous `OnHover()` method, except it is called when the object is pressed. It works with a touch or click. If you need to know which mouse button was used to press the object, use the `UICamera.currentTouchID` variable; if this int is equal to -1, it's a left-click. If it's equal to -2, it's a right-click. Finally, if it's equal to -3, it's a middle-click.

- `OnClick()`: This method is similar to `OnPress()`, except that this method is exclusively called when the click is validated, meaning when an `OnPress(true)` event occurs followed by an `OnPress(false)` event. It works with mouse click and touch.

 You can also use the `OnDoubleClick()` method, which works in the same way.

- `OnDrag(Vector2 delta)`: This method is called at each frame when the mouse or touch moves between the `OnPress(true)` and `OnPress(false)` events. The `Vector2 delta` argument gives you the object's movement since the last frame.

- `OnDrop(GameObject droppedObj)`: This method is called when an object is dropped on the GameObject on which this script is attached. The dropped GameObject is passed as the `droppedObj` parameter.

- `OnSelect()`: This method is called when the user clicks on the object. It will not be called again until another object is clicked on or the object is deselected (click on nothing).

- `OnInput(string text)`: This method is called when the user types in text while an object is selected. The `text` parameter gives the entered text.

- `OnTooltip(bool state)`: This method is called when the cursor is over the object for more than the duration defined by the **Tooltip Delay** inspector parameter of **UICamera**. If the **Sticky Tooltip** Boolean of **UICamera** is checked, the tool tip will remain visible until the cursor moves outside the Collider's Bounds, otherwise the tool tip disappears as soon as the cursor moves.

- `OnScroll(float delta)`: This method is called when the mouse's scroll wheel is moved while the object is hovered – the delta parameter gives you the amount and direction of the scroll.

- `OnKey(KeyCode key)`: This method is called when the user clicks on a key while the object is selected. The pressed key is stored in the `key` parameter.

 If you attach your script on a 3D object to catch these events, make sure it is on a layer included in `Event Mask` of `UICamera`.

Creating a tool tip

Let's now use the OnTooltip() event to show a tool tip for our powers, as shown in the following screenshot:

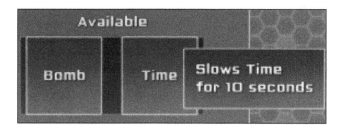

We will also make sure it is localized using methods integrated with NGUI.

The tool tip reference

First, we will create our tool tip that will be shown when needed. These are the steps to do so:

1. Select and duplicate our **Help** GameObject with *Ctrl + D*. Then perform the following steps:

    1. Rename this new duplicate as Tooltip.
    2. Set **Depth** in **UIPanel** to 4.
    3. Set **Clipping** in **UIPanel** to **None**.
    4. Remove its **Box Collider** component.
    5. Remove its **UIDrag** Object component.
    6. Remove its **UIAnchor** component.
    7. Reset its **Transform** position to {0, 0, 0}.

2. Select our new **Background**, which is a child GameObject of **Tooltip**. Then perform the following steps:

    1. Set its **Depth** value to 0.
    2. Set its **Pivot** parameter to **Top Left** (left arrow + up arrow).
    3. Reset its **Transform** position to {0, 0, 0}.
    4. Set its **Dimensions** to 200 x 50.

3. Select **Label**, which is a child GameObject of **Tooltip**. Then perform the following steps:

    1. Set its **Depth** to 1.

    2. Change its text to This is a Tooltip.

    3. Change its **Overflow** parameter to **Resize Height**.

    4. Remove its **Tween Position** component.

    5. Remove its **UILocalize** component.

    6. Set its **Pivot** parameter to **Top Left** (left arrow + up arrow).

    7. Set its **Transform** position to {15, -15, 0}.

    8. Set its **Dimensions** parameter to 200 x 20.

4. Select our **Tooltip** GameObject.

5. Attach a **Tooltip** to the selected object by navigating to **Component | NGUI | UI** and perform the following steps:

    1. Drag our **Label** GameObject from **Tooltip** to its **Text** field.

    2. Drag our **Window** GameObject from **Tooltip** to its **Background** field.

Ok. Our tool tip is ready to be displayed. The fact that we have set the **Pivot** parameter of **Label** under **Tooltip** to **Top left**, with a position of {15, -15, 0}, will force a margin between the text and the background sprite.

The **Overflow** parameter will let the text be resized in height only, which will make our tool tip coherent even if we have a long tool tip — the **Background** sprite will automatically resize to fit the **Label** GameObject.

Showing the tool tip

We must now show the tool tip when needed. In order to do that, we just need to use the OnTooltip() event, in which we will create a new tool tip with localized text.

In the **Project** view, select both our **Time** and **Bomb** prefabs and create and add a new TooltipManager.cs C# script to it.

You can now open this new TooltipManager.cs script and declare the following enum, which will define which type of tool tip it must display:

```
//Enum to define which type of tooltip must be shown
public enum Type
{
```

```
    Bomb,
    Time
}


//Declare the Type enum variable
public Type type;
```

Ok, now add the following `OnTooltip()` method that will create a tool tip with localized text depending on its current type:

```
//When a Tooltip event is triggered on this object
void OnTooltip(bool state)
{
  //If state is true, create a new Tooltip depending on the type
  if(state)
    UITooltip.ShowText(Localization.instance.Get(type.ToString() +
      "Tooltip"));
  //If state is false, hide tooltip by setting an empty string
  else
  UITooltip.ShowText("");
}
```

Save the script. As you can see, we use a useful `Localization.instance.Get(string key)` method that returns localized text of the corresponding `key` parameter that is passed. You can now change a label to localized text through code anytime!

 To use `Localization.instance.Get(string key)`, your label must not have a **UILocalize** component attached to it; otherwise, the value of **UILocalize** will overwrite anything you assign to the label.

Ok, we have added the code to show our tool tip with localized text. Now we have to add these localized strings to the `English.txt` file using the following code:

```
BombTooltip = Explodes all\nenemies at once
TimeTooltip = Slows Time\nfor 10 seconds
```

Similarly, add the following lines in the `French.txt` file:

```
BombTooltip = Détruit tous les ennemis d'un coup
TimeTooltip = Ralentit le temps pour 10 secondes
```

Save these files and go back to Unity to assign the **TooltipManager** type's variables by performing the following steps:

1. In the **Project** view, select our **Bomb** prefab and set its **Type** field in **TooltipManager** to Bomb.

2. In the **Project** view, select our **Time** prefab and set its **Type** field in **TooltipManager** to **Time**.

   Click on the play button. When you leave your cursor on the **Bomb** or **Time** power in the **Available powers** slot, our localized tool tip appears! I actually have the feeling that the delay is too long. Let's correct this.

3. Select our **Camera** GameObject from **UI Root (2D)** and set its **Tooltip Delay** value in **UICamera** to 0.3.

That's better — our localized tool tip appears within 0.3 seconds of hovering.

Tween methods

You can see all available Tweens by simply typing in Tween inside any method in your favorite IDE. You will see a list of Tween classes thanks to autocompletion, as shown in the following screenshot:

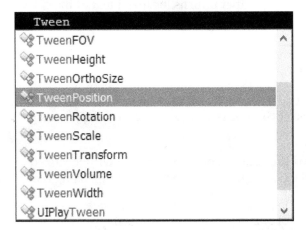

The strong point of these classes is that they work in one line and don't have to be executed for each frame; you just have to call their Begin() method!

Here, we will apply Tweens on widgets since we only have that in the scene. But keep in mind that it works in the exact same way with other GameObjects since NGUI widgets are GameObjects.

Main menu apparition

Let's use the `TweenPosition` class to make our main menu appear from the top of the screen on start. We will first use a simple Tween in only one line and then we will add an easing effect with a delay to make it nicer.

Simple Tween

We can add a **Tween Position** component to our **Container** GameObject in **MainMenu**, but we need to see how we create a **Tween** in code. The following is how we do so:

1. Select our **Container** GameObject from **MainMenu** and create and add a new `AppearFromAbove.cs` C# script to it.

2. Now open this new `AppearFromAbove.cs` script and edit the `Start()` method so that it first sets the `position` value in `Container` to a higher value than the screen's height. Then Tween it back to {0, 0, 0} in 1 second as follows:

```
void Start ()
{
  //First, set the Menu's Y position to be out of screen:
  this.transform.localPosition = new Vector3(0,1080,0);
  //Start a TweenPosition of 1 second towards {0,0,0}:
  TweenPosition.Begin(this.gameObject, 1, Vector3.zero);
}
```

Click on the play button. We now have our main menu coming down from the top of the screen with only two lines of code!

Smooth Tween

We created a simple Tween, but you can also configure your Tween to add a smoothing method and a delay, for example.

Let's try it now by replacing our `Start()` method's code with the following one:

```
void Start ()
{
  //First, set the Menu's Y position to be out of screen
  this.transform.localPosition = new Vector3(0, 1080, 0);
```

```
    //Start a TweenPosition of 1.5 second towards {0,0,0}
    TweenPosition tween = TweenPosition.Begin(this.gameObject, 1.5f,
      Vector3.zero);
    //Add a delay to our Tween
    tween.delay = 1f;
    //Add an easing in and out method to our Tween
    tween.method = UITweener.Method.EaseInOut;
}
```

Click on the play button. We have added a nice EaseInOut method to our Tween. The menu's vertical movement is now smoother, and all of this has been added through code. The following is a list of the different Tween methods that can add effects to Tweens:

- Linear: This will create a simple linear tween—no smoothing
- EaseIn: This will make the tween smooth during the beginning
- EaseOut: This will make the tween smooth during the end
- EaseInOut: This will make the tween smooth both at the beginning and at the end
- BounceIn: This will give the tween bounce effect at the beginning
- BounceOut: This will give the tween bounce effect at the end

Now that you know how to use the TweenPosition class, you are capable of using other Tweens such as TweenScale, TweenRotation, TweenColor or any other available Tween, because they work the same way!

Using keys for navigation

The UI we have created works with the mouse. We can easily add key navigation for keyboard and controllers. A **UIButton Keys** component exists for that purpose. You have to add it to any UI element you want to be accessible with keys (the default **Inspector** window is as follows):

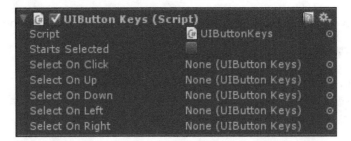

Let's try it now with our **Play**, **Exit**, and **Options** buttons:

1. Select our **Exit**, **Options**, and **Play** GameObjects.

2. Attach a **Button Keys** component to them by navigating to **Component | NGUI | Interaction**.

3. A pop up will appear, as shown in the following screenshot, asking you if you want to replace or add a collider:

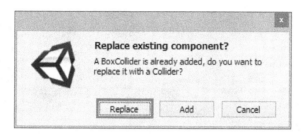

4. That's because they already have a **Box Collider** component. Click on **Replace**.

5. Select the **Play** button and perform the following steps:

   1. Check its **Starts Selected** Boolean.

   2. Drag our **Exit** button into the **Selected On Left** field.

   3. Drag our **Exit** button into the **Selected On Right** field.

   4. Drag our **Options** button into the **Selected On Down** field.

6. Select the **Exit** button and perform the following steps:

   1. Drag our **Play** button into the **Selected On Left** field.

   2. Drag our **Play** button into the **Selected On Right** field.

   3. Drag our **Options** button into the **Selected On Down** field.

7. Select the **Options** button and perform the following steps:

   1. Drag our **Exit** button into the **Selected On Left** field.

   2. Drag our **Play** button into the **Selected On Right** field.

   3. Drag our **Play** button into the **Selected On Up** field.

Click on play. Our **Play** button is selected by default, and if you use your keyboard arrows, you will be able to navigate through those three buttons and validate with *Return*.

Error notification

We want the user to enter a nickname in the input field and select a power before he or she can launch the game.

Right now, the user can launch the game regardless of the input and selected power value. Let's correct this by preventing the game's launch and notifying the user, as shown in the following screenshot:

We will use a TweenScale through code that will gradually scale up the notification from {0, 0, 0} to {1, 1, 1} by following these steps:

1. Select our **Tooltip** GameObject in the **Hierarchy** window.

2. Duplicate it with *Ctrl + D*.

3. Rename this new duplicate as Notification and perform the following steps:

   1. Set its **Depth** parameter in **UIPanel** to 5.

   2. Remove its **UITooltip** component.

   3. Set its **Transform** position to {0, -355, 0}.

4. Select our **Label** GameObject in Notification and perform the following steps:

   1. Change its text to This is a Notification.

   2. Set the **Overflow** parameter to **Shrink Content**.

   3. Set its **Pivot** parameter to **Center** (middle button + middle button).

   4. Set its **Dimensions** to 550 x 80.

   5. Reset its **Transform** position to {0, 0, 0}.

5. Attach a **Localize** component to it by navigating to **Component | NGUI | UI**.

6. Select our **Background** GameObject in `Notification` and perform the following steps:

   1. Set its **Pivot** parameter to **Center** (middle button + middle button).

   2. Reset its **Transform** position to {0, 0, 0}.

   3. Set its **Dimensions** parameters to 600 x 100.

7. Select our **Notification** GameObject and set its **Transform** scale to {0, 0, 1}.

8. Create and attach a new `NotificationManager.cs` C# script to it and open this new `NotificationManager.cs` script.

Ok. We have our **Notification** GameObject ready with a scale of {0, 0, 1}. Let's use the new `NotificationManager.cs` script to launch a TweenScale through code when the **Notification** GameObject is activated.

We will use an enum to define which notification type will be displayed. This time, we will use the **UILocalize** component for localized text and change the `key` parameter through code instead of using the `Localization.instance.Get()` method.

First, declare these variables in the `NotificationManager.cs` script as shown in the following code snippet:

```
//Create an enum to define Notification Type
public enum Type
{
  Nickname,
  Power
}
//Declare necessary variables
public UILocalize loc;
public Type type;
//Store the Notification to access it in static methods
public static NotificationManager instance;
```

Save the script. We will stock the instance of `NotificationManager` on the scene in the script to be able to access it from any other script easily.

First, let's assign our `Loc` variable using the **Inspector** window.

Select our **Notification** GameObject and drag our **Label** GameObject in **Notification** in to the **Loc** field.

Ok, now return to our NotificationManager.cs script. We will first create an Awake() method with our static instance variable's initialization and disable our **Notification** GameObject to make it invisible when the game starts:

```
void Awake()
{
  //Set the static instance to this NotificationManager
  instance = this;
  //Deactivate Notification GameObject on awake
  gameObject.SetActive(false);
}
```

Now that our Awake() method is written, let's create an OnEnable() method that will declare the TweenScale object and set the corresponding key parameter for the UILocalize component as follows:

```
void OnEnable ()
{
  //Start a TweenScale of 0.5 second towards {1, 1, 1}
  TweenScale tween = TweenScale.Begin(this.gameObject, 0.5f, new
    Vector3(1,1,1));
  //Add an easing in and out method to our Tween
  tween.method = UITweener.Method.EaseInOut;
  //Set the Localize key to TypeName + "Notification"
  loc.key = type.ToString() + "Notification";
  //Force Update the UILocalize with new key
  loc.Localize();
}
```

 Don't forget that if you change a key parameter when the **UILocalize** component is already active, you must call its Localize() method to update it.

Good. Click on the play button. Activate our **Notification** GameObject while Unity is running the play mode.

You can see that our **Notification** GameObject appears smoothly. Let's add a Show() method to display it through code as follows:

```
public void Show(Type notificationType, float duration)
{
  //If there is no current Notification
  if(!gameObject.activeInHierarchy)
  {
```

```
      //Set the asked Notification type
      type = notificationType;
      //Enable our Notification on scene
      gameObject.SetActive(true);
      //Start Couroutine to remove in asked duration
      StartCoroutine(Remove(duration));
  }
}
```

The previous method shows our notification by activating its corresponding GameObject. The OnEnable() method will perform the tween and localization.

On its last line, the Show() method starts the Remove() coroutine. Let's add the following Remove() coroutine that will make the notification disappear after a given duration:

```
public IEnumerator Remove(float duration)
{
  //Wait for the Notification display duration
  yield return new WaitForSeconds(duration);
  //Start the TweenScale to disappear
  TweenScale.Begin(gameObject, 0.5f, new Vector3(0,0,1));
  //Wait for 0.5s, the duration of the TweenScale
  yield return new WaitForSeconds(0.5f);
  //Deactivate the Notification GameObject
  gameObject.SetActive(false);
}
```

Great. Now we can add the right localization strings in English.txt as follows:

```
NicknameNotification = [AAFFFF]Please Enter a
  [00FFAA]Nickname[AAFFFF] before you continue!
PowerNotification = [AAFFFF]Please Select a [00FFAA]Power[AAFFFF]
  before you continue!
```

We can also add the correct strings in French.txt as follows:

```
NicknameNotification = [AAFFFF]Merci d'entrer un
  [00FFAA]Pseudo[AAFFFF] avant de continuer !
PowerNotification = [AAFFFF]Merci de sélectionner un
  [00FFAA]Power-Up[AAFFFF] avant de continuer !
```

We can now call our Show() method if the player presses the play button with no nickname entered, or if he or she does not select a power.

In order to do this, we will remove the current **Load Level On Click** component from our **Play** button and attach a new `LaunchValidator.cs` script to it:

1. Select our `Play` button GameObject and remove its **Load Level On Click** component.

2. Create and attach a new `LaunchValidator.cs` C# script to it and open this new `LaunchValidator.cs` script.

In this new script, we will need our nickname's **UIInput** component. Let's declare it as follows:

```
public UIInput nicknameInput;
```

Save the script. Let's assign this variable right now in the **Inspector** window. Then select our **Play** GameObject and drag our **Input** GameObject from **Nickname** in the **Nickname Input** field in its **Launch Validator**.

Go back to our `LaunchValidator.cs` script. We will now add an `OnClick()` method to add a nickname and power validation before we actually load the game, as shown in the following code snippet:

```
void OnClick()
{
  //If the nickname input is empty...
  if(string.IsNullOrEmpty(nicknameInput.value))
  {
    //...Show a Nickname error notification for 2.5 sec
    NotificationManager.instance.Show(NotificationManager.Type.
      Nickname, 2.5f);
  }
  //If there's a nickname but no Power is selected...
  else if(GameManager.SelectedPower == Power.Type.None)
  {
    //...Show a Power error notification for 2.5 sec...
    NotificationManager.instance.Show(NotificationManager.Type.Power,
      2.5f);
  }
  //If there is a nickname AND a Power selected...
  else
  {
    //... Load Game Scene
    Application.LoadLevel("Game");
  }
}
```

Click on the play button. Perfect, we now have notifications that prevent the game from launching if the user has no nickname entered or has no power selected!

Saving the nickname

In *Chapter 2*, *Creating Widgets*, we entered `Nickname` in the **Auto-save Key** parameter of the nickname's **UIInput** component. It works like this: if the user enters a nickname and presses *Return*, the input's label `string` value is saved in the `PlayerPrefs()` method in the `Nickname` key.

Here's the issue: the nickname is saved if, and only if, the user presses *Return*. That's a problem—most of the users will enter a name and select their power directly without pressing *Return*—I'm sure you've done it yourself too.

We need to save the string in the `PlayerPrefs()` method even when the user clicks on the **Play** button without pressing *Return*.

We must add a line at the end of the `OnClick()` method of our `LaunchValidator.cs` script, which will save the nickname's input `value` before the game scene is loaded. Just before the `Application.LoadLevel("Game")` line, add the following:

```
//Save the Nickname to PlayerPrefs before launch
PlayerPrefs.SetString("Nickname", nicknameInput.value);
```

Now the user's nickname is saved before launching the game, no matter what!

Sending messages

The `Notify` parameter in the **Inspector** window we used in previous chapters to call methods on a precise event is usually enough for sending messages. However, you may need to send a message to another GameObject and maybe to its children too.

That's where the **UIButton Message** component comes in handy. We will use this to make our **MainMenu** GameObject scale down before the game actually quits:

1. Select our **Exit** GameObject and perform the following steps:
    1. Attach a **Button Message** component to it by navigating to **Component | NGUI | Interaction**.
    2. Drag our **Container** GameObject from `MainMenu` into its **Target** field.
    3. Type in `CloseMenu` in the **Function Name** parameter.

2. Select our **Container** GameObject in **MainMenu** and open its attached `AppearFromAbove.cs` script.

In this script, add a simple `CloseMenu()` method containing the following lines:

```
void CloseMenu()
{
  //Tween the menu's scale to zero
  TweenScale.Begin(this.gameObject, 0.5f, Vector3.zero);
}
```

Now we need to delay the execution of the `Application.Quit()` method, otherwise we won't see our **Tween**. We do this using the following steps:

1. Select our **GameManager** GameObject and perform the following steps:

    1. Open its attached `GameManager.cs` script.

    2. Replace the line in the `ExitPressed()` method with the following line:

        ```
        //Call the exit function in 0.5s
        Invoke("QuitNow", 0.5f);
        ```

2. Add a new `QuitNow()` method to actually exit the application as follows:

    ```
    void QuitNow()
    {
      Application.Quit();
    }
    ```

    Save the script and click on the play button. When you exit the application, our **Menu** will automatically disappear. That's because the `Invoke()` method enables us to call a function with `delay` as the second parameter.

Let's add this nice scaling effect also when the player launches the game by performing the following steps:

1. Select our **Play** button GameObject and open its attached `LaunchValidator.cs` script.

2. We will need our **Container** GameObject from **MainMenu**. Declare it as follows:

    ```
    public GameObject menuContainer;
    ```

3. Go back to Unity and assign this new **menuContainer** variable as follows:

    1. Select our **Play** button GameObject and drag our **Container** GameObject from **MainMenu** to its **MenuContainer** field.

2. Go back to our `LaunchValidator.cs` script. We simply have to replace the `Application.LoadLevel("Game")` line with the following lines:

```
menuContainer.SendMessage("CloseMenu");
Invoke("LaunchNow", 0.5f);
```

4. Ok, now we can add a new `LaunchNow()` method to actually launch the game scene as follows:

```
void LaunchNow()
{
    Application.LoadLevel(levelName);
}
```

Great, on exit or game launch, the menu scales out, which makes a nicer transition. We have also learned how to use a **UIButton Message** component.

 We didn't need the **Include Children** Boolean checked. But it's interesting to note that you can send a message to the target and all its children at once.

Forwarding an event

Another component may be useful in some cases: **UIForward Events**.
This component gives you the ability to send the events of the GameObject it's attached to to another GameObject in the scene. It can be useful, for example, to create a multiple selection. Let's try it to make it more clear. Perform the following steps:

1. Select our **Bomb** GameObject in **Grid**.

2. Attach a **Forward Events** component to it by navigating to **Component | NGUI | Interaction** and then perform the following steps:

    1. Drag our **Time** GameObject from **Grid** to the `Target` field.

    2. Check the **OnHover** Boolean.

    3. Check the **OnPress** Boolean.

    4. Check the **OnDrag** Boolean.

Click on the play button. If you hover, press, and drag the **Bomb** power, the **Time** power will also react the same way! That is what event forwarding does.

Now that you see how it works, you can remove the **UIForward Events** component from our **Bomb** GameObject.

Summary

In this chapter, we used C# with NGUI to create localized tool tips and error notifications. We learned how to use Tween classes to make our main menu appear and disappear smoothly with methods that ease Tweens.

We also know how to use keys for navigation in our UI, and our nickname is now saved when the game launches. You now know how to send messages and forward events using NGUI components, which may be useful to you in the future.

It's time to create a new `Game.unity` scene and build a complete scrollable viewport, which is the subject of *Chapter 5, Building a Scrollable Viewport*.

5
Building a Scrollable Viewport

In this chapter, we will create a new scene and build a functional scrollable viewport in which we can drop objects that will stick to it. We will add interesting features such as scroll bars and keyboard scrolling with arrows.

This scrollable viewport will be the base of our game from the previous chapter. So, from here, the user will become the player. The idea is that the player can scroll and drag barriers on a viewport, which will take a few seconds to build. Enemies will come down from the top of the screen. If an enemy touches a barrier, he or she will be destroyed along with the barrier—but we will deal with enemies in *Chapter 7, Creating a Game with NGUI*.

The more barriers there are on the scene, the longer the building process will be for the future barriers— this is the same idea with the barriers' cooldown.

Preparing the Game scene

We will need to have our **GameManager** and **Notification** GameObjects as prefabs for this chapter.

From our **Menu** scene, create these two prefabs by dragging them separately in the folder of your choice in the **Project** view.

Now, let's create a new scene with *Ctrl + N* and perform the following steps:

1. Press *Ctrl + S* to save it, and enter Game as the scene's name.
2. In our new scene, delete the **Main Camera** GameObject. We won't need it for this scene.
3. Drag our **GameManager** prefab from the **Project** view into the **Hierarchy** view.
4. Open the **UI Tool** wizard by navigating to **NGUI | Create a New UI**.
5. Add a new **Layer** named Game.

6. Select this **Game** layer for the **Layer** parameter in our **UI Tool** wizard.

7. Click on the **Create Your UI** button.

8. Select our new **Camera** GameObject, and set its **Background Color** to **R**: 0, **G**: 0, **B**: 0, and **A**: 255.

 Make sure your **Color** selector popup is in the **RGBA** values and not **HSVA**. This can be done by using the button next to the **Sliders** option when you click on a **Color** parameter.

9. Select our **UI Root (2D)** GameObject and then perform the following steps:

    1. Set its **Scaling Style** parameter to **FixedSize**.

    2. Set its **Manual Height** to 1080.

Ok, our scene and UI are ready. Your **UI Root (2D)** script should be as shown in the following screenshot:

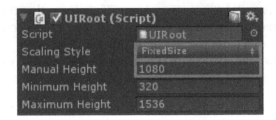

Let's start creating our scrollable viewport.

The scrollable viewport

We will start by creating a clipped, draggable background, and then add linked scroll bars as shown in the following screenshot:

Draggable background

We want the player to be able to scroll on both axes. That means we need a background both larger and taller than the screen size. For this game, we will need quite a large environment to force him or her to scroll regularly. Let's create one that is twice the screen's size.

Perform the following steps to create the environment:

1. Select our **Panel** GameObject and perform the following steps:

    1. Rename it as `Viewport`.

    2. Set its **Clipping** parameter to **Alpha Clip**.

    3. Set its **Clipping Size** to `1920 x 1080`.

2. Add a **Draggable Panel** component to it by navigating to **Component | NGUI | Interaction** and perform the following steps:

    1. Set its **Drag Effect** parameter to **Momentum**. We don't want the player to scroll out of bounds with the spring effect.

    2. Set its **Momentum Amount** value to `10`. Over 10, the background will continue scrolling too much on release.

    3. Set its **Scale** parameter to {1, 1, 0} to enable X and Y scrolling.

3. Attach a **Drag Panel Contents** component to it by navigating to **Component | NGUI | Interaction**.

4. Attach a collider to it by navigating to **NGUI | Attach a Collider**, and set its **Size** to {3840, 2160, 1}.

Now that our **Draggable Panel** is set up, let's add a tiling background as shown in the following screenshot:

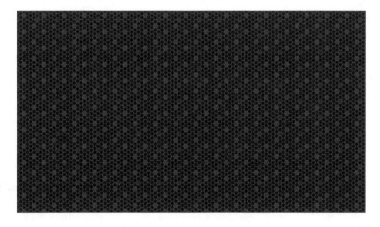

5. Open the **Widget Tool** wizard by navigating to **NGUI | Create a Widget**. Then perform the following steps:

   1. If the **Atlas** field is set to **None**, drag the **SciFi Atlas** prefab in it by navigating to **Assets | NGUI | Examples | Atlases**.

   2. Select the **Sprite** template.

   3. Select the **Honeycomb** sprite.

   4. With our **Viewport** selected; click on the **Add To** button.

6. Select the new **Sprite (Honeycomb)** GameObject and then perform the following steps:

   1. Rename it as Background.

   2. Set its **Sprite Type** to **Tiled**.

   3. Set its **Color Tint** value to {0, 40, 40, 255}.

   4. Set its **Depth** value to 0.

   5. Set its **Dimensions** to 3840 x 2160.

Click on the play button. That's it, we now have a scrollable viewport. You can drag the background by dragging your mouse while clicking.

Linking scroll bars

Let's add scroll bars to know where we are on the viewport. They must be on a separate panel rendered over our viewport, so that they won't move with the draggable background. Perform the following steps to add the scroll bars:

1. Select our **Anchor** GameObject.

2. Create a new child with *Alt + Shift + N* and rename it as UI.

3. Add a **Panel** component to it by navigating to **Component | NGUI | UI**, and set its **Depth** to 1 so that it can be displayed over the viewport.

4. Open the **Widget tool** wizard by navigating to **NGUI | Create a Widget**. Then perform the following steps:

   1. Select **Scrollbar** for the **Template** field.

   2. Select **Dark** sprite as **Background**.

   3. Select **Highlight** sprite as **Foreground**.

   4. Select **Horizontal** for **Direction**.

   5. With our **UI** GameObject selected, click on the **Add To** button.

5. On our **Widget Tool** wizard window, select **Vertical** for **Direction**. With our **UI** GameObject selected, click on the **Add To** button.

We have created both our horizontal and vertical scroll bars at the center of the scene as shown in the following screenshot:

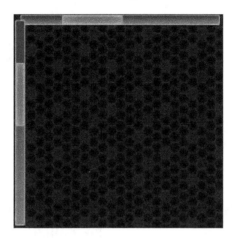

Now, we need to place them correctly and adjust their size to fit the entire screen.

6. Select the vertical **Scroll Bar** GameObject and rename it as VerticalScrollbar.

7. Attach an **Anchor** component to it by navigating to **NGUI | Attach** and perform the following steps:

    1. Drag our **Viewport** GameObject in the **Container** field.
    2. Set its **Side** parameter to **TopRight**.
    3. Set its **Pixel Offset** to {-11, 0}.

8. Select our **Background** GameObject from **VerticalScrollbar**. Then perform the following steps:

    1. Set its **Color Tint** to {130, 255, 245, 110}.
    2. Set the **Center** coordinates of **Box Collider** to {0, -540, 0}.
    3. Set the **Size** of **Box Collider** to {22, 1080, 0}.

9. Attach a **Stretch** component to it by navigating to **Component | NGUI | UI**.

    1. Set its **Style** parameter to **Vertical**.
    2. Set its **Relative Size** values to {1, 0.983} in order to leave space for our horizontal scroll bar at the bottom of the screen.

10. Select the **Foreground** GameObject from **VerticalScrollbar**, and set its **Color Tint** to {0, 255, 128, 255}.

    Our vertical scroll bar is configured. Let's do the same for the horizontal scroll bar.

11. Select the horizontal **Scroll Bar** GameObject, and rename it as HorizontalScrollbar.

12. Attach an **Anchor** component to it by navigating to **NGUI | Attach**. Then perform the following steps:

    1. Drag our **Viewport** GameObject into the **Container** field.

    2. Set its **Side** parameter to **BottomLeft**.

    3. Set its **Pixel Offset** to {0, 11}.

13. Select our **Background** GameObject from **HorizontalScrollbar** and perform these steps:

    1. Set its **Color Tint** to {130, 255, 245, 110}.

    2. Set the **Center** coordinates of **Box Collider** to {960, 0, 0}.

    3. Set the **Size** of **Box Collider** to {1920, 22, 0}.

14. Attach a **Stretch** component to it by navigating to **Component | NGUI | UI**, and set its **Style** parameter to **Horizontal**.

15. Select the **Foreground** GameObject from **HorizontalScrollbar**, and set its **Color Tint** to {0, 255, 128, 255}.

Good. Both our horizontal and vertical scroll bars are set up. Now, we need to assign them to our scrollable viewport by performing the following steps:

1. Select our **Viewport** GameObject.

2. Drag our **HorizontalScrollbar** GameObject from **UI** to the **Horizontal Scroll Bar** field in **UIDraggable Panel**.

3. Drag our **VerticalScrollbar** GameObject from **UI** to the **Vertical Scroll Bar** field in **UIDraggable Panel**.

4. Change the **Show Scroll Bars** parameter to **Always**.

Click on the play button. That's it. Our scroll bars can be used to scroll, and they indicate where we are on the viewport as we scroll. Your hierarchy should be as shown in the following screenshot:

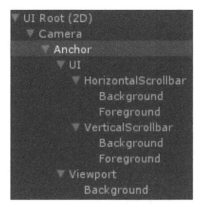

Now, let's add keyboard scrolling.

Keyboard scrolling

For this game, scrolling with the keyboard is important. In order to do so, we will create a custom script that will force our scroll bars to move depending on the pressed key. Select our **Viewport** GameObject, and attach a new `KeyboardScroll.cs` script to it. Open this new script, and declare the required variables and the `Awake()` method:

```
//We need the Scrollbars for keyboard scroll
UIScrollBar hScrollbar;
UIScrollBar vScrollbar;
public float keyboardSensitivity = 1;

void Awake()
{
  //Assign both scrollbars on Awake
  hScrollbar =
    GetComponent<UIDraggablePanel>().horizontalScrollBar;
  vScrollbar = GetComponent<UIDraggablePanel>().verticalScrollBar;
}
```

Okay, we have both of our scroll bars on `Awake()`, and a float value for sensitivity.

Now, let's check the horizontal and vertical input axes at each frame, and change our scroll bars' values consequently:

```
void Update()
{
  //Get keyboard input axes values
  Vector2 keyDelta = Vector2.zero;
  keyDelta.Set(Input.GetAxis("Horizontal"),
    Input.GetAxis("Vertical"));
  //If no keyboard arrow is pressed, leave
  if(keyDelta == Vector2.zero) return;
  //Make it framerate independent and multiply by sensitivity
  keyDelta *= Time.deltaTime * keyboardSensitivity;
  //Scroll by adjusting scrollbars' values
  hScrollbar.value += keyDelta.x;
  vScrollbar.value -= keyDelta.y;
}
```

Save the script and click on the play button. You can now scroll using the keyboard arrows. You may also adjust the **Sensitivity** parameter in the **Inspector** window as you see fit.

Now, it's time to create draggable barriers that we can drop inside our **Viewport** GameObject.

Creating draggable barriers

It is time to create our draggable barriers. The player will be able to drag-and-drop the **BarrierObject** prefab in the **Viewport** GameObject. This **BarrierObject** prefab will look as shown in the following screenshot:

The BarrierObject prefab

First, we need to create our **BarrierObject** prefab's holder that will contain the draggable object:

1. Select our **UI** GameObject.

2. Create a new child with *Alt + Shift + N* and rename it as `Barrier`.

3. Open the **Widget Tool** wizard by navigating to **NGUI | Open** and perform the given steps:

    1. Select **Sprite** for the **Template** parameter.
    2. Select **Dark** sprite for the **Sprite** field.
    3. With our **Barrier** GameObject selected, click on the **Add To** button.

4. Select our new barrier's **Sprite (Dark)** GameObject and perform the following steps:

    1. Rename it as `Background`.
    2. Set its **Sprite Type** to **Sliced**.
    3. Set its **Color Tint** to {0, 250, 250, 170}.
    4. Set its **Depth** value to 0.
    5. Set its **Dimensions** to 200 x 200.

5. Select our **Barrier** GameObject.

6. Attach a collider to it by navigating to **NGUI | Attach a Collider** and perform the following steps:

    1. Set its **Center** coordinates in **Box Collider** to {0, 0, 0}.
    2. Set the **Size** parameter of **Box Collider** to {200, 200, 1}.

7. Attach **Anchor** to it by navigating to **NGUI | Attach**.

    1. Drag our **Viewport** GameObject in its **Container** field.
    2. Set its **Side** parameter to **TopLeft**.
    3. Set its **Pixel Offset** to {100, -100}.

Ok, we have our **BarrierObject** holder's background at the top left-hand corner as shown in the following screenshot:

Let's create the actual **BarrierObject** prefab, which will be a custom button:

1. Select our **Barrier** GameObject.

2. Open the **Widget tool** wizard by navigating to **NGUI | Create a Widget** and perform the following steps:

    1. Drag the **SciFi Font – Normal** prefab into the **Widget Tool** wizard's **Font** field by navigating to **Assets | NGUI | Examples | Atlases | SciFi**.

    2. Select **Button** for the **Template** field.

    3. Select the **Highlight** sprite for the **Background** field.

    4. With our **Barrier** GameObject selected, click on the **Add To** button.

3. Select our new **Button** GameObject from **Barrier**.

    1. Rename it as `BarrierObject`.

    2. Set its **Center** coordinates **Box Collider** to {0, 0, 0}.

    3. Set **Size** of **Box Collider** to {160, 160, 0}.

4. Drag the **Background** GameObject from **BarrierObject** into the **Target** field in **UIButton**. Then perform the following steps:

    1. Set its **Normal Color** to {125, 255, 155, 130}.

    2. Set its **Hover Color** to {100, 255, 60, 255}.

    3. Set its **Pressed Color** to {20, 255, 0, 160}.

    4. Set its **Disabled Color** to {115, 115, 155, 255}.

5. Select the **Background** GameObject from **BarrierObject** and perform the following steps:

    1. Set its **Depth** value to 1.

    2. Set its **Dimensions** to 160 x 160.

6. Select the **Label** GameObject from **BarrierObject** and then perform the given steps:

    1. Set its text to [99FF99]Barrier.

    2. Set its **Depth** to 2.

Ok. We now have our **BarrierObject** in the **Barrier** holder. Let's make it draggable by performing the following steps:

1. Select our **BarrierObject** GameObject.

2. Attach a **Drag Object** component to it by navigating to **Component | NGUI | Interaction**.

   1. Drag our **BarrierObject** GameObject in its **Target** field.

   2. Set its **Scale** parameter to {1, 1, 0} to avoid Z scrolling.

   3. Set its **Drag Effect** parameter to **None**. We want it to be precise.

3. Create and attach a new `BarrierObjectController.cs` C# script to it.

Click on the play button. The **BarrierObject** prefab is now draggable. Now, it is time to handle the drop on the **Viewport** GameObject.

Before we continue, drag our **BarrierObject** in a folder of your choice in the **Project** view to make it a prefab.

Dropping a barrier on Viewport

In order to drop a barrier inside the **Viewport** GameObject, we need to catch the **Viewport** GameObject's `OnDrop()` event and check what was dropped:

1. Select our **Viewport** GameObject.

2. Create and attach a new `ViewportHolder.cs` C# script to it.

3. Open this new `ViewportHolder.cs` script.

In this script, we can add a new `OnDrop()` method that will be called when an object is dropped on it:

```
void OnDrop(GameObject droppedObj)
{
  //Get the dropped object's BarrierObjectController
  BarrierObjectController barrierObj =
    droppedObj.GetComponent<BarrierObjectController>();

  //If it actually has one, destroy the droppedObj
  if(barrierObj != null){
    Destroy(droppedObj);
  }
}
```

Save the script and click on the play button. Surprisingly, when you drop the **BarrierObject** on the **Viewport** GameObject, nothing happens!

That's because, like in *Chapter 3, Enhancing your UI*, the Collider of **BarrierObject** is enabled when the OnPress(false) event occurs. This obstructs the collision detection of **UICamera**.

We just have to disable the collider while dragging, and re-enable it when dropping it. Let's also make it reposition itself if it isn't dropped on the **Viewport** GameObject. Open our BarrierObjectController.cs script, and add following OnPress() method to do so:

```
void OnPress(bool pressed)
{
  //Invert the Collider's state
  collider.enabled = !pressed;

  //If it has just been dropped
  if(!pressed)
  {
    //Get the target's collider
    Collider col = UICamera.lastHit.collider;
    //If the target has no collider or is not the viewport
    if(col == null || col.GetComponent<ViewportHolder>() == null)
    //Reset its localPosition to {0,0,0}
    transform.localPosition = Vector3.zero;
  }
}
```

Save the script and click on the play button. This time, the collider is disabled when the **BarrierObject** prefab is dropped. So, it is indeed dropped on the collider of **Viewport** and destroyed instantly.

If it is dropped somewhere else (out of screen or on the barrier's container), it is automatically replaced at the center of the barrier's container. Let's make this **BarrierObject** a prefab by dragging it in the folder of your choice inside the **Project** view.

We can now create an **ActiveBarrier** prefab that will be instantiated on the **Viewport** GameObject.

Creating an ActiveBarrier prefab

When a **BarrierObject** is dropped on the **Viewport** GameObject, we want
to instantiate an **ActiveBarrier** prefab that will take a few seconds to build,
using a slider as status indicator as shown in the following screenshot:

The ActiveBarrier prefab

Let's create the **ActiveBarrier** prefab by performing the following steps:

1. Select our **Viewport** GameObject.

2. Create a new child with *Alt + Shift + N*.

3. Select this new child and rename it as `ActiveBarrier`.

4. Open the **Widget Tool** wizard by navigating to **NGUI | Create a Widget**
   and perform the following steps:

    1. Select **Progress Bar** for the **Template** field.

    2. Set **Dark** sprite as **Empty**.

    3. Set the **Highlight** sprite as **Full**.

    4. With our **ActiveBarrier** GameObject selected, click on the
       Add To button.

A **Progress Bar** has just been created as child of the **ActiveBarrier**
GameObject as shown in the following screenshot:

It doesn't look like anything. Let's configure it to look like an **ActiveBarrier** prefab by performing the following steps:

1. Select our new **Background** GameObject from **Progress Bar** and perform the following steps:
    1. Uncheck its **Fill Center** boolean to only keep edges.
    2. Set its **Color Tint** to {100, 200, 100, 255}.
    3. Set its **Depth** to 1 so that it can be rendered over the **Viewport** background.
    4. Set its **Dimensions** to 160 x 160.

2. Select our **Foreground** GameObject from **Progress Bar** and perform the following steps:
    1. Set its **Color Tint** to {75, 190, 95, 255}.
    2. Set its **Depth** value to 2.
    3. Set its **Dimensions** to 160 x 160.

3. Select our **Progress Bar** from **ActiveBarrier** and perform the following steps:
    1. Rename it as Slider.
    2. Set its **Transform Position** to {-80, 0, 0} to center it.
    3. Set the **UISlider** value to 0 to make sure it's empty at start.

4. Select our **ActiveBarrier** GameObject.

5. Attach a collider to it by navigating to **NGUI | Attach**, and set its **Size** to {160, 160, 1}.

The slider of **ActiveBarrier** GameObject is ready. If you click on the play button and change the **Slider** value in the **Inspector** view during runtime, you will see the **ActiveBarrier** prefab building itself.

Let's add a label that will show the status of **ActiveBarrier**: either **Building** or **Built**.

1. Duplicate our **Label** GameObject in **BarrierObject** and perform the following steps:
    1. Drag it inside our **ActiveBarrier** GameObject.
    2. Reset its **Transform Position** to {0, 0, 0}.
    3. Set its **Depth** to 3.
    4. Add a Localize component to it by navigating to **Component | NGUI | UI**.
    5. Set the key of **UILocalize** to BuildingBarrier.

2. Drag our **ActiveBarrier** in the folder of your choice inside the **Project** view to make it a prefab.

3. Delete the **ActiveBarrier** instance from the scene.

Ok, our **ActiveBarrier** prefab is ready. Now, add the following localization strings to English.txt:

```
//Game
Barrier = [99FF99]Barrier
BuildingBarrier = [FF6666]Building\nBarrier...
Wait = Wait
```

Also, add the following localization strings to French.txt:

```
//Game
Barrier = [99FF99]Barrière
BuildingBarrier = [FF6666]Construction\nBarrière...
Wait = Attendez
```

Now, everything is set for our **ActiveBarrier** prefab.

Instantiating the ActiveBarrier prefab

Now that we have our prefab, we need to instantiate it when a **BarrierObject** prefab is dropped inside the **Viewport** GameObject.

Open our ViewportHolder.cs script and declare our necessary variables:

```
//We need our two barriers Prefabs
public Object barrierObjectPrefab;
public Object activeBarrierPrefab;

//We need the BarrierObject container
public GameObject barrierContainer;
```

Save the script. Let's go back to the scene and assign these variables in the **Inspector** view:

1. Select the **Viewport** GameObject.

2. Drag the **BarrierObject** prefab from the **Project** view in the **BarrierObject** prefab field of **Viewport Holder**.

3. Drag the **ActiveBarrier** prefab from the **Project** view in the **ActiveBarrier** prefab field **Viewport Holder**.

4. Drag the **Barrier** GameObject in **UI** from the **Hierarchy** view to the **Barrier Container** field in **Viewport Holder**.

The necessary variables are assigned. Go back to our `ViewportHolder.cs` script, and add the following two lines to call the appropriate methods, after `Destroy(droppedObj)`:

```
RecreateBarrierObject();
CreateActiveBarrier(droppedObj.transform);
```

Now, we can add these two methods that will recreate our **BarrierObject** prefab. Also, we can add an **ActiveBarrier** prefab to the **Viewport** GameObject:

```
void RecreateBarrierObject()
{
  //Add a BarrierObject to the container
  Transform newBarrierTrans = NGUITools.AddChild(barrierContainer,
    barrierObjectPrefab as GameObject).transform;
  //Reset its localPosition to {0,0,0}
  newBarrierTrans.localPosition = Vector3.zero;
}

void CreateActiveBarrier(Transform barrierObjectTrans)
{
  //Add an ActiveBarrier to the Viewport
  Transform newActiveBarrierTrans = NGUITools.AddChild(gameObject,
    activeBarrierPrefab as GameObject).transform;
  //Set position to the droppedObject's position
  newActiveBarrierTrans.position = barrierObjectTrans.position;
}
```

Click on the play button. When you drag the **BarrierObject** prefab onto the **Viewport** GameObject, it creates our **ActiveBarrier** prefab; and it recreates a **BarrierObject** prefab to be able to drag another one.

Barrier's building process

Right now, our dropped **ActiveBarrier** instances stay empty and never build. Let's make them fill themselves at a speed depending on the number of barriers in the scene:

1. Select our **ActiveBarrier** prefab in the **Project** view.
2. Create and add an `ActiveBarrierController.cs` script to it.

Open this new `ActiveBarrierController.cs` script, and add these necessary variables and the `Awake()` method to initialize them:

```
//We will need the Slider and the Label's UILocalize
private UISlider slider;
private UILocalize loc;

void Awake()
{
  //Get necessary components at Awake()
  slider = GetComponentInChildren<UISlider>();
  loc = GetComponentInChildren<UILocalize>();
}
```

Now that we have our necessary variables initialized, let's add a coroutine that will increase the **UISlider** value over time, at a rate depending on a given `buildTime`:

```
public IEnumerator Build(float buildTime)
{
    while(slider.value < 1) {
    slider.value += (Time.deltaTime / buildTime);
    yield return null;
    }
    //When slider value is > 1
    BuildFinished();
}
```

Ok. Let's add the `BuildFinished()` method that will set the **Slider** value to 1 (in case this value is higher), and change the **UILocalize** key:

```
private void BuildFinished()
{
  //Make sure it's at 1
  slider.value = 1;
  //Set the key to "normal" barrier and update Localization
  loc.key = "Barrier";
  loc.Localize();
}
```

Good. We just need to edit the `ViewportHolder.cs` script to add a `barrierCount` variable, and start the new `Build()` coroutine from **ActiveBarrier**.

Open the `ViewportHolder.cs` script and declare a new `int` after our `barrierContainer`:

```
public int barrierCount = 0;
```

Now, let's add these two simple lines of code to update the `barrierCount` variable and start the `Build()` coroutine on our new **ActiveBarrier** prefab:

```
//Update barrierCount
barrierCount++;
//Start the Build Coroutine with the correct buildTime
StartCoroutine(newActiveBarrierTrans.GetComponent
  <ActiveBarrierController>().Build(barrierCount *2));
```

Click on the play button. Now, our **ActiveBarrier** prefab builds itself depending on the number of **ActiveBarriers** on the scene!

Forwarding events to viewport

You may have noticed that you cannot scroll if you click on an **ActiveBarrier** prefab. That's because it catches the events instead of our viewport.

Let's simply forward its events to the viewport:

1. Select our **ActiveBarrier** prefab in the **Project** view.
2. Attach a **Forward Events** component to it by navigating to **Component | NGUI | Interaction** and perform the following steps:

    1. Check its **On Press** Boolean.
    2. Check its **On Drag** Boolean.

3. Open the `ActiveBarrierController.cs` script that is attached to it.

We need to assign the target variable of the **UIForward Event** component when the **ActiveBarrier** prefab is created. To do so, add a new `Start()` method with the following:

```
void Start()
{
  //Set the UIForwardEvents' target to the viewport
  GetComponent<UIForwardEvents>().target =
    transform.parent.gameObject;
}
```

We can now scroll no matter what. We are missing something: a cooldown on the BarrierObjects that also depends on the number of ActiveBarriers.

BarrierObject cooldown

We will implement the cooldown system that will deactivate the **BarrierObject** button as shown in the following screenshot:

Then, we will make the barrier's apparition smoother by tweening its scale.

Cooldown implementation

In order to implement the required cooldown, we need to open the `BarrierObjectController.cs` script and add the following two necessary variables with an initialization on `Awake()`:

```
//We will need the Button and the Label
private UIButton button;
private UILabel label;

void Awake()
{
  //Get necessary components at Awake
  button = GetComponentInChildren<UIButton>();
  label = GetComponentInChildren<UILabel>();
}
```

Now that we have the button and label, we can add a `Cooldown()` coroutine that will deactivate the button and update the label to show the remaining time to the player:

```
public IEnumerator Cooldown(int cooldown)
{
  //Deactivate the Barrier button and update Color to Disable
  button.isEnabled = false;
  button.UpdateColor(false, true);
```

```
while(cooldown > 0)
{
  //Update Label with localized text each second
  label.text = Localization.instance.Get("Wait") + " " +
    cooldown.ToString() + "s";
  cooldown -= 1;
  //Wait for a second, then return to start of While
  yield return new WaitForSeconds(1);
}
//If cooldown <= 0
CooldownFinished();
}
```

The previous coroutine updates the label and decreases the cooldown. We can now add the `CooldownFinished()` method that will reactivate the button and reset the label:

```
void CooldownFinished()
{
  //Reset the Label's Text to "normal" Barrier
  label.text = Localization.instance.Get("Barrier");
  //Reactivate the Barrier button and update Color to Normal
  button.isEnabled = true;
  button.UpdateColor(true, true);
}
```

Great, everything is ready for our cooldown. We just need to start the `Cooldown()` coroutine when a new **BarrierObject** prefab is created.

In order to do this, let's go back to our `ViewportHolder.cs` script and add the following line at the very end of the `RecreateBarrierObject()` method:

```
//Start the new BarrierObject's Cooldown Coroutine
StartCoroutine(newBarrierTrans.GetComponent
  <BarrierObjectController>().Cooldown((barrierCount +1) *3));
```

Perfect. Here, we needed to pass `barrierCount +1` as argument because at this stage it is not yet updated (it is incremented in the `CreateActiveBarrier()` method).

Click on the play button. When you drop a **BarrierObject** prefab on the **Viewport** GameObject, you will only be able to drop another one when the cooldown is finished. The more barriers you have, the longer the cooldown.

BarrierObject smooth apparition

Let's add a TweenScale to make the barrier's availability more obvious to the player. Go back to our `BarrierObjectController.cs` script and add the following two lines at the very end of the `CooldownFinished()` method:

```
//Set its scale to {0,0,0}
transform.localScale = Vector3.zero;
//Tween it back to make it appear smoothly
TweenScale.Begin(gameObject, 0.3f, new Vector3(1,1,1));
```

That's better. Now, the animated apparition of **BarrierObject** attracts the player's eye. But, hey, we created a notification in the previous chapter. Let's reuse it to make it even more obvious!

The barrier availability tool tip

Let's set up notifications in the game using our previous work:

1. Drag our **Notification** prefab inside our **UI** GameObject.

2. Select the new **Notification** GameObject in the **Hierarchy** view, and then perform the following steps:

    1. Change its **Layer** to **Game** (in the top right-hand corner of the **Inspector** view).

    2. A pop up will appear. Click on **Yes**, and change children.

    3. Open the `NotificationManager.cs` script that is attached to it.

First, we need to add a new notification type. This is done by adding a third line to our type enum:

```
BarrierAvailable
```

Now, add the following localization string to `English.txt`:

```
BarrierAvailableNotification = New [99FF99]Barrier[FFFFFF]
    Available!
```

Also, add the following localization string to `French.txt`:

```
BarrierAvailableNotification = Nouvelle [99FF99]Barrière[FFFFFF]
    Disponible !
```

Everything is set. Now, go back to our `BarrierObjectController.cs` script, and add the following line of code at the very end of the `CooldownFinished()` method:

```
//Show Notification to inform the player
NotificationManager.instance.Show(NotificationManager.Type.Barrier
    Available, 1.5f);
```

Click on the play button. A localized notification will appear as soon as a new barrier is available. This way, we are sure that the player will not miss it.

Summary

In this chapter, we learned how to create a scrollable viewport using a scrollable background. Also, we linked the mouse drag, scroll bars, and keyboard arrows to it.

We used the **UIDrag Object** component to create our drag-and-drop system, allowing us to drag objects inside the scrollable viewport.

Coroutines helped us to create the barriers' building process and cooldown system. The **UIForward Events** component was used to forward events to the viewport. Finally, we reused our **Notification** prefab inside our new **Game** scene.

We now have the basic elements for *Chapter 7, Creating a Game with NGUI*. Now, it is time to discover how to add sprites and fonts to NGUI with *Chapter 6, Atlas and Font Customization*. We will then use our own assets to create a game!

Atlas and Font Customization

6

In this chapter, we will learn how to create a new atlas and add our own assets. At the end of this chapter, you will know how to handle normal, sliced, and tiled sprites.

We will use these new assets to add icons to our powers and selected powers. We will also change the backgrounds of our different windows, and add a new font to our project.

A small exercise will let you customize your main menu as you see fit before we move on to the final chapter. First, we need to learn how to create our own **Game** atlas.

The Atlas prefab

With NGUI, an Atlas prefab is used to contain sprites and fonts. It is composed of the following:

- A large texture file containing all sprites and fonts
- A material with this texture file assigned, and a specific shader

The Atlas prefab has a **UIAtlas** component attached to it. Its purpose is to contain information about your sprites' positions and sizes in the large texture.

It is much more efficient to use only one large texture that holds all our sprites, instead of having separate multiple small textures.

Creating a new Atlas

Let's create our own Atlas to hold our sprites and new fonts. First, open our **Menu** scene. In order to do this, we will use the **Atlas Maker** wizard.

Navigate to **NGUI | Atlas Maker**, or press *Alt + Shift + M* to bring up the following screen:

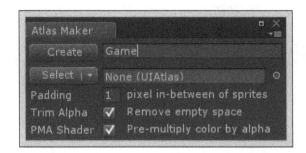

To create the Atlas, perform the following steps:

1. In the first field, type in the new atlas' name as Game.

2. Click on the green **Create** button.

Our new **Game** atlas has been created, and it is selected in the **Atlas Maker** wizard. It is empty for now. Let's change this.

 You may have as many Atlases as you want, but remember that rendering multiple Atlases simultaneously will increase the number of draw calls.

Adding sprites to Atlas

Let's add some sprites to our new **Game** atlas. We will add the following three different types:

- **Simple** sprite: As its name suggests, it is simply an image displayed on screen

- **Sliced** sprite: In this, the image is sliced in nine parts and it is resizable without stretching corners

- **Tiled** sprite: In this, the tiling pattern is repeatable indefinitely

Let's start with the **Simple** sprites.

Simple sprites

It is time to create two sprites, Bomb and Time, which will illustrate our powers. First, we need to create the sprites and add them to our **Game** atlas. They will look as shown in the following screenshot:

 You may either create them yourself, or download the `Assets.zip` file from `http://goo.gl/bZu4mF`.

If you wish to create your own sprites, a size of 128 x 128 will be enough. You can save them either as `.png` to support transparency, or as `.psd` files—they will be converted to the correct format when they will be imported in the Unity project.

Adding sprites to Atlas

When your Bomb and Time sprites are ready, or downloaded from the previous link, place them in a new `Assets/Textures` folder in your project. Then, perform the following steps:

1. Open **Atlas Maker** from **NGUI**, or *Alt + Shift + M*.

2. Make sure that our new **Game** Atlas is selected, as shown in the following screenshot:

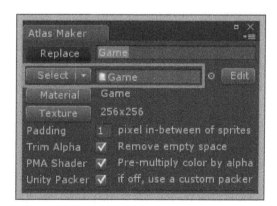

3. In the **Project** view, select both our new **Bomb** and **Time** textures.

4. Click on the **Add/Update All** button in **Atlas Maker**.

Good. Our two new sprites have been added to the **Game** atlas.

Available powers icons

Let's add the icons to our **Time** and **Bomb** prefabs on the scene and perform the following steps:

1. In the **Hierarchy** view, select **Background** by navigating to **PowersContainer | Grid | Bomb** and perform the following steps:

    1. Duplicate it.

    2. Rename this new duplicate as Icon.

    3. Change its **Sprite Type** parameter in **UISprite** to **Simple**.

    4. Set its **Depth** to 6 so that it can be displayed over the background.

2. Click on the **Atlas** button in **UISprite** and in the pop-up window, select our new **Game** atlas.

 If the new **Game** Atlas is not visible in the list, drag it from the **Project** view in the field next to the **Atlas** button.

3. Click on the **Sprite** button in **UISprite** and in the pop-up window, select our **Bomb** sprite.

4. Select the **Label** GameObject from **Bomb** and perform the following steps:

    1. Delete it—the icon and tool tip are enough!

    2. A pop-up window appears, asking you if you want to continue because you will lose the prefab connection. Click on **Continue**.

5. Select the **Bomb** GameObject from our **Grid**.

6. Click on the **Apply** button in the **Inspector** view to update the prefab.

Good, our **Bomb** prefab is up to date with its new icon. Let's add the icon for the **Time** prefab by performing the following steps:

1. Select our **Icon** GameObject **Bomb** and perform the following steps:
    1. Duplicate it.
    2. Drag this duplicate inside the **Time** GameObject.
    3. Reset its **Transform** position to {0, 0, 0}.
    4. Change its **Sprite** parameter to our own **Time** sprite.
    5. Change its **Dimensions** to 75 x 75.

2. Select the **Label** GameObject from **Time** and then perform the following steps:
    1. Delete it—the icon and tool tip are enough!
    2. A pop-up window appears, asking you if you want to continue because you will lose the prefab connection. Click on **Continue**.

3. Select the **Time** GameObject from **Grid**.

4. Click on the **Apply** button in the **Inspector** view to update the prefab.

Ok, our draggable powers prefabs now have their own icons.

Selected powers icons

Let's also add icons for our **SelectedBomb** and **SelectedTime** prefabs so that they look nicer:

Perform the following steps to achieve this:

1. From the **Project** view, drag the **SelectedBomb** prefab in our **Surface** GameObject.

2. In the **Hierarchy** view, select our **Icon** GameObject from **Grid/Bomb** and perform the given steps:
   1. Duplicate it.
   2. Drag this duplicate inside our new **SelectedBomb** instance.
   3. Reset its **Transform** position to {0, 0, 0}.
   4. Set its **Depth** to 5.
   5. Change its **Dimensions** to 120 x 120.

3. Select the **Label** GameObject from **SelectedBomb** and delete it.

4. Select the **SelectedBomb** GameObject from **Surface** and perform the given steps:
   1. Click on the **Apply** button in the **Inspector** view to update the prefab.
   2. Delete the **SelectedBomb** instance from the scene.

Let's follow the same steps for our **SelectedTime** prefab:

1. From the **Project** view, drag the **SelectedTime** prefab in our **Surface** GameObject.

2. In the **Hierarchy** view, select our **Icon** GameObject from **Time** and perform the following steps:
   1. Duplicate it.
   2. Drag this duplicate inside our new **SelectedTime** instance.
   3. Reset its **Transform** position to {0, 0, 0}.
   4. Set its **Depth** to 5.
   5. Change its **Dimensions** to 100 x 100.

3. Select the **Label** GameObject from **SelectedTime**, and delete it.

4. Select the **SelectedTime** GameObject from **Surface** and perform the following steps:
   1. Click on the **Apply** button in the **Inspector** view to update the prefab.
   2. Delete the **SelectedTime** instance from the scene.

That's it. We have our own two icons for our powers. Now, we can learn how to create and configure our own nine-sliced sprite.

Sliced sprites

We used the dark sliced sprite all along this book. Let's create our own. Then, we will change the power selection box and the background sprites of **Main Menu**, as shown in the following screenshot:

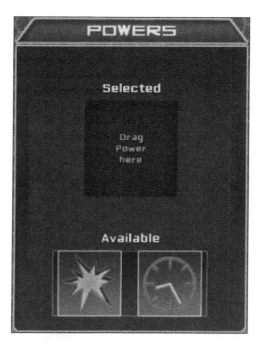

Adding a sprite to Atlas

You can use a 16 x 16 square sprite, such as the dark sprite. If you wish to have larger corners or add more details, simply use a larger texture size. You can also use the 64 x 64 Window.png file available in my Assets.zip archive.

When your new Window sprite is ready, place it in the Assets/Textures folder and perform the following steps:

1. Open **Atlas Maker** by navigating to **NGUI | Atlas Maker**, or *Alt + Shift + M* and make sure our new **Game** atlas is selected.
2. Select the new Window.png sprite file from **Textures** in the **Project** view.
3. Click on the green **Add/Update All** button in the **Atlas Maker** window.

Ok, Window.png has been added to our **Game** atlas, but it isn't configured. Yet.

Configuring a sliced sprite

The Window sprite has been added to the atlas, but we still need to indicate the **UIAtlas** component where the slicing must occur on the sprite. Let's replace our **Background** of **Powers**, and configure its slicing parameters.

In the **Hierarchy** view, select the **Background** GameObject from **Powers** and perform the following steps:

1. Change its **Atlas** parameter in **UISprite** to our **Game** Atlas.

2. Change its **Sprite** to our new **Window** sprite.

3. Click on the **Edit** button next to the **Sprite** field, as shown in the following screenshot:

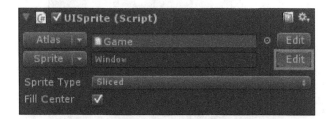

We are now in the sprite's parameter window. Here, we can configure its **Dimensions**, **Border**, and **Padding**. Set these **Border** values to define the slicing lines:

The values shown in the previous screenshot might be different if you created your own sprite.

[As you change the **Border** values, dotted lines appear on the sprite at the bottom of the **Inspector** view in the **Preview** window.]

The **Window** sprite should be sliced (as shown in the following screenshot) in the **Preview** window:

When you have entered your four values, you can click on the green **Return to Background** button in order to go back to where we were.

We now have a functional sliced sprite, but we need to adjust the title position of the powers. In the **Hierarchy** view, select our **TitleLabel** GameObject from **Powers**, and change its **Pixel Offset** in **UIAnchor** to {0, -18}.

Good! We configured our first sliced sprite and changed the power selection box's background sprite with it.

The Main Menu window

Let's change our **Window** sprite **Main Menu** too. In the **Hierarchy** view, select our **Window** GameObject from **Container** and perform the following steps:

1. Change its **Atlas** to our **Game** Atlas.
2. Change its **Sprite** to our new **Window** sprite.

The **Main Menu** title is not placed exactly inside the title bar. Let's change this by performing the following steps.

1. Select the **Title** GameObject from **Container**, and change its **Pixel Offset** value in **UIAnchor** to {0, 10}.

2. Select the **Background** GameObject from **Title** and deactivate it for now.

3. Select the **Background** GameObject from **Container** and then perform the following steps:

    1. Change its **Relative Size** in **UIStretch** to {1, 0.95}.

    2. Change its **Pixel Offset** in **UIAnchor** to {0, -17}.

Great. That looks better. If you wish, you may change the nickname box's background sprites with our new Window sprite. You can even change the buttons by using the sliced sprite Button.png included in the Assets.zip file.

> The Button.png file can be used for non-button backgrounds too, such as the notification or tool tip backgrounds. Try it out!

Tiled sprites

Let's add a tiled sprite to create a space background for our **Game** scene.

You can use the Space.jpg file from the Assets.zip archive, or you may create a 256 x 256 tiling sprite representing stars in space. Place the Space.jpg sprite in the Assets/Textures folder, and then perform the following steps:

1. Open our **Game** scene.

2. Open **Atlas Maker** by navigating to **NGUI | Atlas Maker**, or *Alt + Shift + M*. Then perform the following steps:

    1. In the **Project** view, select our new Space.jpg file from **Textures**.

    2. Click on the **Add/Update All** button of the **Atlas Maker** window.

Ok, the new Space.jpg sprite has now been added to our **Game** Atlas. Let's change our **Game** scene's background to make it look like we're in space.

1. Select the **Background** GameObject from **Viewport**.

2. Change its **Atlas** to our **Game** Atlas.

3. Change its **Sprite** to our new **Space** sprite.

4. Change its **Color Tint** to {140, 200, 200, 255}.

That's it! Small stars are now tiling in the background. Now, it is time to add a font.

Adding a font

For optimization, NGUI uses bitmaps instead of true type fonts. We need to export our .ttf or .otf fonts to a bitmap using a free third-party tool called **BMFont**, which was created by **AngelCode**.

Then, we will need a .txt file that will contain information about where each glyph is located in the exported font's bitmap. You can download the BMFont from www.angelcode.com/products/bmfont/. Free-to-use fonts are available at www.openfontlibrary.org/.

For our first font, we will use the Pacaya font created by *Daniel Johnson* — it is included in the Assets.zip archive. Download, install, and launch BMFont. Install the font now by right-clicking on the Pacaya.otf file and then selecting **Install**.

Exporting a font using BMFont

Once BMFont is launched and the Pacaya font is installed, go to **Options | Font Settings**. You can now select the Pacaya font in the **Font** field. The **Size(px)** field defines the font's size at export in pixels — set it to 24 and click on **OK**.

Our .otf file is loaded, and we can visualize and select the characters that we want to export with a left-click or click-and-drag. Select them all with *Ctrl + A*.

 If you want to export a selection of characters, don't forget to select the empty character — it's your space character.

Go to **Options | Export** options. Here, you must set the **Bit** depth to 32. Now, the only thing you need to check is the **Width** and **Height** value of the bitmap.

To see if it's currently big enough, click on **OK** and go to **Options | Visualize**. The window shown in the following screenshot appears:

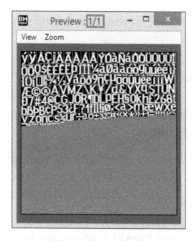

The red space represents wasted space. As you can see, we have a large amount of wasted space. You must try to set the bitmap size to reduce this red space as much as possible, while making sure you have enough space for all characters.

If your bitmap size is too small and can't hold all your characters, the **Preview** window's title will show **Preview : 1/2** instead of **Preview : 1/1**, as shown in the following screenshot. Then, you should increase the bitmap size utile it displays **Preview : 1/1**. For the Pacaya font with all characters selected, enter 256 x 128. It should look as shown in the following screenshot:

 For optimization, you should keep its dimensions as powers of two.

Once you have set the correct bitmap size, go back to **Options | Export Options**. Then, make sure the **Presets** field is set to **White text with alpha** in order to have **R**, **G**, and **B** channel values at **one** and the **glyph** in channel **A**:

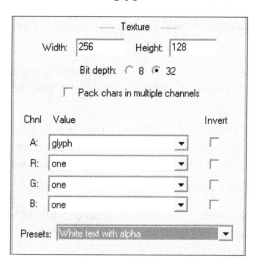

When you've done that, go to **Options | Save bitmap font as...** and name it `Pacaya`. The `.fnt` file extension will be added automatically. Inside the output folder you selected, you should have a `Pacaya_0.tga` file—the actual font bitmap—and a `.fnt` file.

You must have only one `.tga` file along with your `.fnt` file. Otherwise, your bitmap size is too small, and you need to make it larger before you re-export.

Ok, now copy these two files in a new `Assets/Fonts/Sources` folder.

Creating a font in Unity

We have our new font files. We must now create a new font for NGUI using these files.

In Unity, perform the following steps:

1. Open the **Font Maker** window by navigating to **NGUI | Font Maker**, or *Alt + Shift + F*.

2. In the **Project** view, browse to your `Assets/Fonts/Sources` folder.

3. Drag your `Pacaya.fnt` file in the **Font Data** field in **Font Maker**.

4. Drag the `Pacaya_0.tga` file in the **Texture** field in **Font Maker**.

5. Enter `Pacaya` in the **Font Name** field.

6. Click on the **Atlas** button and choose our **Game** Atlas.

 This means the font's texture will be added to the **Game** Atlas, resulting in no supplementary draw call when a label is displayed.

7. Select any file in the `Sources` folder in the path `Assets/Fonts/` of our **Project** view—our font will then be added to the current folder, but you need to actually select a file inside the desired destination for it to work.

8. Click on the green **Create the Font** button.

A new Pacaya prefab has been created in the `Sources` folder in the path `Assets/Fonts/`. That's the prefab NGUI needs to display the font.

Select it in the **Project** view, and drag it inside our `Fonts` folder in `Assets`. If you cannot find it, simply type your font's name in the **Project** view's search bar.

Assigning a new font to Label

Now that we have added a new font to our project, let's assign it to a Label:

1. Open our **Menu** scene.

2. Select our **Label** GameObject by navigating to **MainMenu | Container | Nickname | Input** and perform the following steps:

    1. Click on the **Font** button in **UILabel**.

    2. Choose our new **Pacaya** font.

 If the new font does not appear in recent fonts, find it in your **Project** view and drag it manually in the **Font** field in **UILabel**.

Ok. We have added a new font to our project and assigned it to a label!

Customizing the MainMenu

The blue background of our menu's main camera is not very nice. Let's set a black background for the camera, and add our space tiling sprite to make this better:

1. Select our **MainMenu** GameObject from **Anchor**, and create a new sprite by navigating to **NGUI | Create | Sprite**, or press *Alt + Shift + S*.

2. Select the new **Sprite** GameObject from **MainMenu** and perform the following steps:

    1. Rename it as `Space`.

    2. Set its **Atlas** type to our **Game** atlas.

    3. Set its **Sprite** to our **Space** tiling sprite.

    4. Set its **Sprite Type** parameter to **Tiled**.

3. Attach a **Stretch** component to it by navigating to **Component | NGUI | UI**:

4. Set its **Style** parameter to **Both**.

You may notice that we have ugly lines between each repetition of the Space sprite. That is simply because there is a 1-pixel-wide border on the sprite. We can easily correct this by reducing the sprite's border value of 1 pixel.

Select our **Space** GameObject from **MainMenu**, and click on the **Edit** button next to the **Sprite** field, as shown in the following screenshot:

Set a value of 1 for each of the four **Border** parameters as shown in the following screenshot:

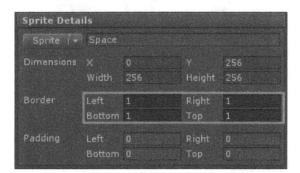

That's better; our tiling sprite now tiles correctly without any lines between each pattern.

Now that you have learned how to add sprites and fonts, I would like you to change our **Main Menu** elements' backgrounds to make it look better. You may proceed as you wish—add more sprites if you want, change colors, and use your imagination!

The following is an example of what you can achieve with the **Window** and **Button** sprites:

 You might have to move or resize the UI elements. Don't forget to use **Pixel Offset** in **UIAnchor** to move or resize instead of positions. Same for **Dimensions**—don't use the scale tool of Unity if you want to keep the widgets pixel perfect.

Summary

In this chapter, we learned how to create a new Atlas and add simple, sliced, and tiled sprites. Using these new sprites, we made our **Powers**, **Selected Powers**, and **Main Menu** windows look better than before.

You now know how to use BMFont to export a font as bitmap and create a new font prefab for NGUI.

Before we move on to the final *Chapter 7, Creating a Game with NGUI*, you should have changed the appearance of your **Main Menu** to make it look nicer.

7

Creating a Game with NGUI

In this final chapter, we will create a game using NGUI elements, and this will ensure that you understand them and know how to use them perfectly.

Together, we will learn how to create these basic game rules, which are as follows:

1. Enemies fall down from the top of our scrollable viewport.
2. The player drops Barriers on the Viewport—if the enemy collides with a built Barrier, he or she is destroyed along with the Barrier.
3. Some enemies have encrypted self-destruct code. The player clicks on the enemy to hack it. When the hacking process is complete, its destruct code is displayed above it.
4. The player must type in the code to destroy the enemy.

We will also add a health bar that will represent the player's health points and will decrease when enemies hit the bottom of the screen. The game will look as follows:

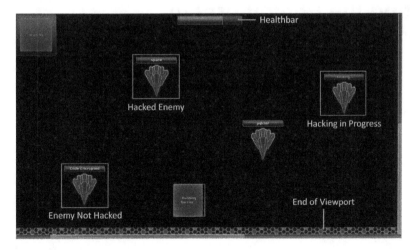

Enemy spawning

We want our enemies to spawn at the top of the viewport's background. At spawn, the Y value can be the same for each of the enemies, but we want a random X value.

First of all, let's open our **Game** scene.

Creating the enemies container

Our enemies will be nested in a container placed at the top left-hand corner of our background in order to have the {0, 0} positioned at the top left-hand corner of the viewport.

First, let's create our enemies holder by performing the following steps:

1. Select our **Viewport** GameObject and perform the following steps:

   1. Create a new child by pressing *Alt + Shift + N*.

   2. Rename this new child as Enemies.

2. Attach **Anchor** to it by navigating to **NGUI | Attach**. Then perform the following steps:

   1. Drag our **Background** from Viewport into the **Container** field.

   2. Set its **Side** parameter to **TopLeft**.

Ok, we now have our enemies container in which we will instantiate our **Enemy** prefab.

Creating the Enemy prefab

Let's create the **Enemy** prefab that will be instantiated as child of the **Enemies** GameObject. You must add the Enemy.png file included in the Assets.zip file to the **Game** atlas before you continue or you may create your own 128 x 160 sprite. We will use a **Rigidbody** to detect collisions between the enemies and our barriers.

Once the Enemy.png sprite has been added to the **Game** atlas, follow the given steps:

1. Select our **Viewport** GameObject and perform the following steps:

   1. Create a new child with *Alt + Shift + N*.

   2. Rename this new child as Spaceship.

2. Select our new **Spaceship** GameObject.

3. Attach a collider to it by navigating to **NGUI | Attach a Collider** and perform the following steps:

    1. Uncheck its **Is Trigger** Boolean to detect collisions.

    2. Set **Size** to {128, 160, 1}.

4. Attach a **Rigidbody** component to it by navigating to **Component | Physics** and then perform the following steps:

    1. Uncheck its **Use Gravity** Boolean.

    2. Check its **Is Kinematic** Boolean.

    3. Check the **Freeze Position** and **Freeze Rotation** Booleans for all its **Constraints** in order to avoid any unwanted behavior.

5. With our selected **Spaceship** GameObject, create a new **Sprite** by navigating to **NGUI | Create | Sprite**:

    1. Change its **Sprite** to our new **Enemy** sprite.

    2. Change its **Dimensions** to 128 x 160.

    3. Set its **Depth** to 1.

6. Drag our **Spaceship** GameObject in your Prefabs folder.

7. Delete our **Spaceship** instance from the scene.

Ok, we now have our **Enemy** prefab ready. Let's add a new script to it that will handle the enemy's initialization and movement, and perform the following steps:

1. In the **Project** view, select our **Spaceship** prefab.

2. Create and attach a new EnemyController.cs C# script to it.

3. Open this new EnemyController.cs script.

Let's create a new Initialize() method that will set the enemy's position outside the game with a random X and a tween duration depending on the float value that is passed as a parameter in the following manner:

```
public void Initialize(float _movementDuration)
{
  //Get the Viewport's Background size
  Vector2 bgSize =
    transform.parent.parent.FindChild("Background").GetComponent
      <UISprite>().localSize;
  //Get this enemy's sprite size
  Vector2 spriteSize =
```

```
        transform.FindChild("Sprite").GetComponent<UISprite>().localSize;
    //Set its position to a random X, and Y of -(enemyHeight/2)
    transform.localPosition =
        new Vector3(Random.Range(spriteSize.x *0.5f, bgSize.x -
            (spriteSize.x *0.5f)), -(spriteSize.y *0.5f), 0);
    //Tween its position towards end of background
    TweenPosition.Begin(gameObject, _movementDuration,
        new Vector3(transform.localPosition.x, -bgSize.y +
            (spriteSize.y * 0.5f), 0));
}
```

We used `spriteSize.x * 0.5f` in the preceding code because our enemy has a centered pivot and we want to avoid spawning it outside the background's width.

The `_movementDuration` parameter is used to define how much time the enemy will take to cross our entire background; it is used as speed. But to balance the speed, a value of 10 is used, which means that the enemy will need 10 seconds to hit the bottom of the background.

At this stage, your hierarchy should look as follows:

Creating the enemy spawn controller

Before we can launch the game, we need to add an `EnemySpawnController.cs` script that will handle enemy spawn rates and instantiate enemies when needed. To add the script, perform the following steps:

1. Select the **Enemies** GameObject from **Viewport**.

2. Create and attach a new `EnemySpawnController.cs` C# script.

3. Open this new `EnemySpawnController.cs` script.

In this new script, we need to add a `SpawnEnemy()` coroutine that will be called at random intervals to instantiate **Enemy** prefabs and initialize them with the correct position and tween duration. First, we need to declare these variables as shown in the following code snippet:

```
//We need our Enemy Prefab for Instantiation
public Object enemyPrefab;
//Random-control variables
public int firstEnemyDelay = 1;
//Min and Max intervals between 2 spawns
public float minInterval = 4;
public float maxInterval = 15;
//Min and Max Enemy MovementTime
public float minMovementTime = 20;
public float maxMovementTIme = 50;
```

The variables declared in the previous code will be used to control our random values. You may change them in the **Inspector** view. We need to assign our `enemyPrefab` variable.

To do this, go back to Unity and follow the given steps:

1. Select the **Enemies** GameObject from **Viewport**.

2. Drag our **Spaceship** prefab from the **Project** view inside the **Enemy Prefab** field in **Enemy Spawn Controller**.

Ok, the necessary variables are initialized. Now, let's go back to our `EnemySpawnController.cs` script and add a new `SpawnEnemy()` coroutine by using the following code snippet:

```
//Coroutine that spawns enemies
IEnumerator SpawnEnemy()
{
  //First time, set to firstEnemyDelay
  float delay = firstEnemyDelay;
  //Loop while the game is running
  while(true){
    //Wait for the correct delay
    yield return new WaitForSeconds(delay);
    //Create a new enemy, stock its EnemyController
    EnemyController newEnemy =
      NGUITools.AddChild(gameObject, enemyPrefab as
        GameObject).GetComponent<EnemyController>();
    //Initialize it with random speed
```

```
    newEnemy.Initialize(Random.Range (minMovementTime,
      maxMovementTIme));
    //Set the new random delay
    delay = Random.Range(minInterval, maxInterval);
  }
}
```

Our coroutine is ready. Let's start it when the game starts running. We can use the
`Start()` method for this. Add this method just below our `SpawnEnemy()` coroutine
in the following manner:

```
void Start ()
{
  //Start the Spawn Coroutine with first delay
  StartCoroutine(SpawnEnemy());
}
```

Save the script and click on the play button. The first enemy is spawned after the
`firstEnemyDelay`. After the first enemy, new enemies are spawned at random X
positions, at random intervals, and at a random speed.

Your **Hierarchy** view should look as follows when a few enemies have spawned:

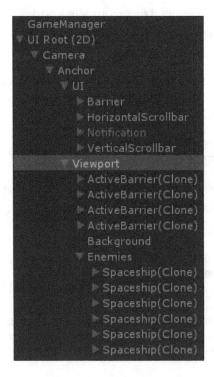

Spawned enemies move down and stop at the end of the Viewport's background as shown in the following screenshot:

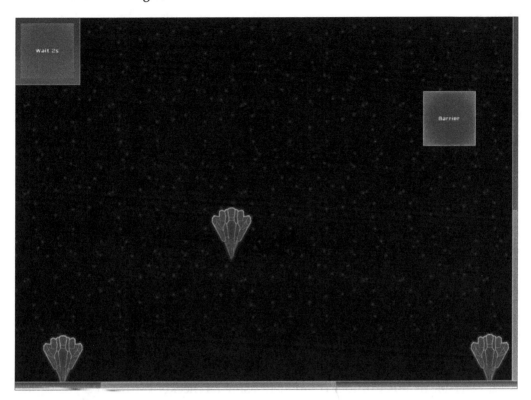

Forwarding events to viewport

Ok, we now have our mobile enemies, but we still have a slight problem. You may have noticed that you cannot drag the viewport if you click on an enemy. We had the same problem before with the **ActiveBarrier** prefab.

We need to add a **UIForwardEvents** component to the **Spaceship** prefab by performing the following steps:

1. In the **Project** view, select our **Spaceship** prefab.
2. Attach a **Forward Events** component to it by navigating to **Component | NGUI | Interaction**. Then perform the following steps:
    1. Check its **OnPress** Boolean.
    2. Check its **OnDrag** Boolean.
3. Open its attached `EnemyController.cs` script.

Add the following line at the end of the `Initialize()` method of `EnemyController.cs` script:

```
//Set the Viewport as target for UIForwardEvents
GetComponent<UIForwardEvents>().target =
    transform.parent.parent.gameObject;
```

You can now pan the viewport even if you click on an enemy. It is time to handle collisions with barriers.

Handling enemy collisions

We need to handle collisions between our enemies and ActiveBarriers. Since we have a Rigidbody attached to our **Enemy** prefab, it will receive the `OnTriggerEnter()` event when it hits the collider of an **ActiveBarrier** GameObject.

Once the collisions with ActiveBarriers are implemented, we'll add collisions with the bottom of the screen, which will reduce the player's health.

Collisions with active barriers

First of all, we must disable the ActiveBarrier's collider by default and enable it when the barrier is built in the following manner:

1. In the **Project** view, select our **ActiveBarrier** prefab.

2. Disable its **Box Collider** component using its checkbox.

3. Open the `ActiveBarrierController.cs` script attached to it.

4. We will need a new `built` boolean that will help us know if the barrier has finished its building process. Along with our `UISlider` and `UILocalize` variables, declare the following:

   ```
   private bool built = false;
   ```

5. Now, add the following two lines at the end of the `BuildFinished()` method:

   ```
   //Set the build value to true and activate collider
   built = true;
   collider.enabled = true;
   ```

6. Ok, now the collider is enabled only when the barrier is built. We can add a `HitByEnemy()` method with the concerned `enemy` passed as a parameter that will destroy the barrier and the enemy in the following manner:

```
public void HitByEnemy(EnemyController enemy)
{
  //If the barrier isn't built, don't go further
  if(!built) return;
  //Else, kill the enemy
  StartCoroutine(enemy.Kill());
  //Kill the barrier too
  StartCoroutine(RemoveBarrier());
}
```

7. Here, we start two coroutines: one to kill the enemy and another one to remove the barrier. Let's add the `RemoveBarrier()` coroutine now with the following code snippet:

```
IEnumerator RemoveBarrier()
{
  //Tween for smooth disappearance
  TweenScale.Begin(gameObject, 0.2f, Vector3.zero);
  //Notify the Viewport that a Barrier has been removed
  transform.parent.SendMessage("BarrierRemoved");
  //Wait for end of tween, then destroy the barrier
  yield return new WaitForSeconds(0.2f);
  Destroy(gameObject);
}
```

The coroutine in the previous code scales down the barrier before it is destroyed. We send a message to the parent (**Viewport**) because we need to decrease the `barrierCount` value.

8. Let's add the `BarrierRemoved()` method in the `ViewportHolder.cs` script. In the **Hierarchy** view, select our **Viewport** GameObject and open the `ViewportHolder.cs` script attached to it.

9. In our `ViewportHolder.cs` script, add the following new `BarrierRemoved()` method:

```
void BarrierRemoved()
{
  //Decrease the barrierCount value
  barrierCount--;
}
```

10. The `barrierCount` value will be updated as soon as a barrier is destroyed. Now, let's open the `EnemyController.cs` script and add the `Kill()` coroutine as shown in the following code snippet:

```
public IEnumerator Kill()
{
    //Tween for smooth disappearance
    TweenScale.Begin(gameObject, 0.2f, Vector3.zero);
    //Deactivate the collider now
    collider.enabled = false;
    //Wait end of tween, then destroy the enemy
    yield return new WaitForSeconds(0.2f);
    Destroy(gameObject);
}
```

11. Great! All of our coroutines and methods are ready. Now, we need to call the `HitByEnemy()` method of the concerned **ActiveBarrier** when a collision occurs.

12. We just have to add the following `OnTriggerEnter()` method inside our `EnemyController.cs` script, which will call this method only if the collided object actually is a barrier:

```
void OnTriggerEnter(Collider other)
{
    //Store the collided object's ActiveBarrierController
    ActiveBarrierController barrierController =
        other.GetComponent<ActiveBarrierController>();
    //If it has a BarrierController, call HitByEnemy
    if(barrierController != null)
    barrierController.HitByEnemy(this);
}
```

13. Save all of the scripts and click on the play button.

If you place a barrier on an enemy's trajectory, both of them will be destroyed when they collide! If the building process isn't over, nothing happens.

In the case where a barrier finishes its building process while an enemy is still inside it, a collision will occur. Perfect!

Now that the player can destroy his or her enemies, let's add a way for the enemies to destroy the player.

Colliding with the bottom of the screen

We can now add a collider at the bottom of the viewport's background that will destroy enemies and reduce the player's health. Before we do this, let's create a Healthbar with a HealthController script.

Healthbar

To create this Healthbar, we need the Button.png file available in the Assets.zip file. If you haven't added it to the **Game** Atlas as a sliced sprite yet, please do so before you continue.

We will use a Progress Bar to create a Healthbar on which we will add a HealthController.cs script to handle the display of damage and health points. Perform the following steps to do so:

1. In the **Hierarchy** view, select the **UI** GameObject from **Anchor**.
2. Open the **Widget Tool** window by navigating to **NGUI | Create a Widget**. Then perform the following steps:
    1. Select our **Game** Atlas.
    2. Select the **Progress Bar** template.
    3. Select our **Button** sprite for the **Empty** field.
    4. Select our **Button** sprite for the **Full** field.
    5. With our **UI** GameObject selected, click on the **Add To** button.
3. Select the new **Progress Bar** GameObject and rename it as Healthbar.
4. Attach an **Anchor** to it by navigating to **NGUI | Attach**. Then perform the following steps:
    1. Drag our **Viewport** GameObject in the **Container** field.
    2. Set the **Side** parameter to **Top**.
    3. Set **Pixel Offset** to {-160, -30}.
5. Select the **Background** GameObject from **Healthbar** and perform the following steps:
    1. Set **Color Tint** to {255, 120, 120, 140}.
    2. Set **Dimensions** to 320 x 42.
    3. Change **Sprite Type** to **Sliced**.
    4. Click on the **Edit** button next to the **Sprite** field.
    5. Set all four border values to 6 for slicing parameters.

6. Select the **Foreground** GameObject from **Healthbar** and then perform the following steps:

   1. Set **Color Tint** to {25, 245, 255, 255}.

   2. Set **Dimensions** to 320 x 42.

   3. Change **Sprite Type** to **Sliced**.

Ok, we have a configured health bar centered at the top of the screen. We need to add a script to it that will handle health points and modify the value of **Slider** accordingly. The steps to do so are as follows:

1. In the **Hierarchy** view, select our **Healthbar** GameObject.

2. Create and add a new HealthController.cs script to it.

3. Open this new HealthController.cs script.

In this new script, we will save a static reference to the instance of the HealthController class so that its methods are easily accessible from other scripts. First, let's declare necessary variables and initialize them on Awake() as shown in the following code:

```
//Static variable that will store this instance
public static HealthController Instance;
//We will need the attached slider and a HP value
private UISlider slider;
private float hp = 100;

void Awake()
{
  //Store this instance in the Instance variable
  Instance = this;
  //Get the slider Component
  slider = GetComponent<UISlider>();
}
```

Ok, our variables are now initialized correctly. Let's create a Damage() method that will reduce the hp value and update the slider as follows:

```
public void Damage(float dmgValue)
{
  //Set new HP value with a clamp between 0 and 100
  hp = Mathf.Clamp(hp - dmgValue, 0, 100);
  //Update the slider to a value between 0 and 1
```

```
    slider.value = hp * 0.01f;
    //If hp <= 0, restart level
    if(hp <= 0)
    Application.LoadLevel(Application.loadedLevel);
}
```

Great! The `Damage()` method is ready. Let's create the **EndOfScreen** widget that will collide with the enemies.

The EndOfScreen widget

Let's create the **EndOfScreen** widget that will help detect enemy collisions as follows:

1. In the **Hierarchy** view, select our **Viewport** GameObject and perform the following steps:

    1. Create a new child by pressing *Alt + Shift + N*.

    2. Rename this new child as `EndOfScreen`.

2. Attach a collider to it by navigating to **NGUI | Attach a Collider** and set **Size** to {3840, 43, 1}.

3. Attach **Anchor** to it by navigating to **NGUI | Attach**.

    1. Drag the **Background** GameObject from **Viewport** in the **Container** field.

    2. Set its **Side** parameter to **Bottom**.

    3. Set its **Pixel Offset** to {0, 33}.

4. Click on the **Untagged / Add Tag...** button at the top of the **Inspector** view.

5. Create a new `DamageZone` tag.

6. Select our **EndOfScreen** GameObject.

7. Set **Tag** to **DamageZone**.

8. Make sure our **EndOfScreen** GameObject is selected.

9. Create a new sprite by navigating to **NGUI | Create | Sprite** and perform the following steps:

    1. Set its **Atlas** type to the **SciFi** Atlas.

    2. Set its **Sprite** type to the **Honeycomb** sprite.

    3. Set its **Sprite Type** to **Tiled**.

4. Set its **Color Tint** values to **R**: 255, **G**: 120, **B**: 120, and **A**: 255.

5. Set its **Depth** value to 2.

6. Set its **Dimensions** parameter to 3840 X 43.

Good. We now have an **EndOfScreen** limit with a sprite and a collider. Now, we need to edit our EnemyController.cs script's OnTriggerEnter() method to check if the collided object has the **DamageZone** tag and hurt the player if needed. Perform the following steps to do so:

1. In the **Project** view, select our **SpaceShip** prefab and open the EnemyController.cs script attached to it.

2. Within the EnemyController.cs script, at the very first line of the OnTriggerEnter() method, add the following lines to check if the collided object has a **DamageZone** tag:

```
//Is the collided object a DamageZone?
if(other.CompareTag("DamageZone"))
{
  //In that case, hurt the player
  HealthController.Instance.Damage(30f);
  //Then, kill the enemy and don't go further
  StartCoroutine(Kill());
  return;
}
```

3. Save all of the scripts and click on the play button. Now, our enemies are destroyed when they collide with the end of the Viewport, and the player's health is decreased!

Now, let's add another way to destroy our enemies.

Creating self-destruct code

Dropping barriers on the screen is not enough. We will use a self-destruct code to destroy enemies too.

Each enemy will get a chance to have a self-destruct code. If it has one, an empty slider with **Code Encrypted** displayed inside it will appear above the concerned enemy.

When the player clicks on the enemy, the hacking process starts. When the hacking is complete, a word will appear as shown in the following screenshot, and the player will have to type it on his keyboard to destroy it:

The hacking slider

Let's start by creating the hacking slider indicator inside our **Spaceship** prefab by performing the following steps:

1. In the **Project** view, select our **Spaceship** prefab.
2. Drag it in the **Hierarchy** view as child of the **Viewport** GameObject.
3. Open the **Wiget Tool** window by navigating to **NGUI | Create a Widget** and then perform the following steps:
    1. Select the **Game** Atlas.
    2. Select the **Progress Bar** template.
    3. Select the **Button** sprite for the **Empty** field.
    4. Select the **Button** sprite for the **Full** field.
4. With our **Spaceship** instance selected, click on the **Add To** button.
5. Select the new **Progress Bar** GameObject and perform the following steps:
    1. Rename it as DestructCode.
    2. Set its **Transform** position to {-100, 100, 0}.
    3. Set the value of **UISlider** to 0.
6. Select the **Background** GameObject from **DestructCode**. Then perform the following steps:
    1. Change its **Color Tint** values to {255, 140, 140, 255}.
    2. Set its **Depth** value to 2.

7. Select the **Foreground** GameObject from **DestructCode** and then perform the given steps:

    1. Change **Color Tint** to {50, 180, 220, 255}.

    2. Set its **Depth** value to 3.

Ok, the slider is ready. Let's add a label that will display **Code Encrypted** and will change to the self-destruct code when the hacking process is finished.

1. In the **Hierarchy** view, select our **DestructCode** GameObject.

2. Open the **Widget Tool** window by navigating to **NGUI | Create a Widget** and perform the given steps:

    1. Select the **SciFi Font – Normal** font.

    2. Select the **Label** template.

    3. Change the **Color** to **R**: 255, **G**: 215, **B**: 190, and **A**: 255.

3. With the **DestructCode** GameObject selected, click on the **Add To** button.

4. Select the new **Label** GameObject from **DestructCode** and perform the following steps:

    1. Set its **Transform** position to {100, 0, 0}.

    2. Set its text to Code Encrypted.

Your **Hierarchy** view and **Spaceship** should look as follows:

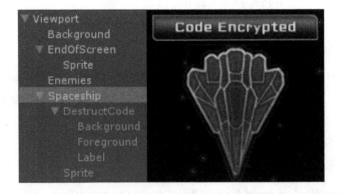

Great! Let's apply these new modifications to our **Spaceship** prefab by performing the following steps:

1. In the **Hierarchy** view, select our **Spaceship** GameObject.
2. Click on the **Apply** button at the top of the **Inspector** view to update the prefab.
3. Delete the **Spaceship** instance from our **Hierarchy** view.

Ok, we now have a slider that will indicate the hacking status and a label that will display the self-destruct code.

Self-destruct code

Let's add some self-destruct code and hacking status in the localization files. Open the English.txt and add the following lines:

```
//Hacking status
CodeEncrypted = Code Encrypted
Hacking = [FF6666]Hacking...
//Self-Destruct Codes
Space = space
Neptune = neptune
Moon = moon
Mars = mars
Jupiter = jupiter
```

Now, open the French.txt file and add the following lines:

```
//Hacking status
CodeEncrypted = Code Crypté
Hacking = [FF6666]Piratage...
//Self-Destruct Codes
Space = espace
Neptune = neptune
Moon = lune
Mars = mars
Jupiter = jupiter
```

Good! We now have our necessary localization strings.

Assigning code to an enemy

We will now add a new `SetDestructCode()` method in our `EnemyController.cs` script that will assign a self-destruct code to our enemy during initialization. First, let's add the necessary global variables to it.

Open our `EnemyController.cs` script and add the following global variables:

```
//Boolean to check if enemy is hacked or not
public bool hacked = false;
//We will need the Self-Destruct Code Label
private UILabel codeLabel;
//We will also need the hacking slider
private UISlider hackSlider;
//We will need to store the destructCode
public string destructCode = "";
//We will need a hackSpeed float
float hackSpeed = 0.2f;
```

We must set these variables. Add the following lines at the end of the `Initialize()` method:

```
//Get the hacking slider
hackSlider =
  transform.FindChild("DestructCode").GetComponent<UISlider>();
//Get the hacking status label
codeLabel =
  hackSlider.transform.FindChild("Label").GetComponent<UILabel>();
```

Ok, now, let's add the `SetDestructCode()` method that will assign a self-destruct code to the enemy. This method will have a string parameter containing the key of the self-destruct code to be assigned, as shown in the following code:

```
public void SetDestructCode(string randomWordKey)
{
  //If the randomWordKey is not empty...
  if(!string.IsNullOrEmpty(randomWordKey))
  {
    //... Get the corresponding localized code
    destructCode = Localization.instance.Get(randomWordKey);
    //Set the Label to "Code Encrypted"
    codeLabel.text = Localization.instance.Get("CodeEncrypted");
  }
  //If the randomWordKey is empty, disable hacking slider
  else
  hackSlider.gameObject.SetActive(false);
}
```

Ok, we have a method that sets the correct destruct code. Now, let's create a `Hack()` coroutine that will be called to start the hacking process.

The hacking process

The `Hack()` coroutine will gradually fill the hacking slider and display the enemy's self-destruct code when the hacking is complete.

Add the `Hack()` coroutine to the `EnemyController.cs` script using the following code snippet:

```
IEnumerator Hack()
{
  //Set the Label to "Hacking..."
  codeLabel.text = Localization.instance.Get("Hacking");
  //While hacking slider is not full
  while(hackSlider.value < 1)
  {
    //Increase slider value, framerate independant
    hackSlider.value += Time.deltaTime * hackSpeed;
    //Wait for next frame
    yield return null;
  }
  //Make sure slider is at 1
  hackSlider.value = 1;
  //Set the hacked bool to true for this enemy
  hacked = true;
  //Display the Self-Destruct code now
  codeLabel.text = "[99FF99]" + destructCode;
}
```

Now, let's add an `OnClick()` method that will actually launch the hacking process when the enemy is clicked on by the player. We do this in the following manner:

```
void OnClick()
{
  //If the enemy has a destruct code, launch hacking
  if(!string.IsNullOrEmpty(destructCode))
    StartCoroutine(Hack());
}
```

Ok, the methods are set for our enemy. Now, we can edit our `EnemySpawnController.cs` script to call the `SetDestructCode()` method when a new enemy is initialized and pass a random destruct code in parameter. First, we will add the necessary variables.

We will need a `List` array to store the enemies in the scene. A `List` is like an array but easier to manage with useful methods, such as `Add()` and `Remove()`. In order to use a `List`, you need to include a specific library.

Open the `EnemySpawnController.cs` script and simply add the following line at the very beginning of the file, along with the two other include lines already present:

```
//Include Lists
using System.Collections.Generic;
```

Now, add these new global variables within our `EnemySpawnController` class:

```
//Chance for each enemy to have a destructCode
public float destructCodeChance = 60;
//Array of strings to store destructCodes keys
public string[] wordKeys;
//We will need a list of enemies
private List<EnemyController> enemies;
//We will need a static instance of this script
public static EnemySpawnController instance;
//This will store the current word typed by the player
public string currentWord;
```

Ok, now initialize some of these variables in the new `Awake()` method:

```
void Awake()
{
  //Store the instance of this script
  instance = this;
  //Initialize the List
  enemies = new List<EnemyController>();
}
```

Before we continue, let's assign the remaining variables in the **Inspector** view. Save the script, go back to Unity, and select our **Enemies** GameObject from **Viewport**.

Now, set the **Word Keys** array and spawning values as follows:

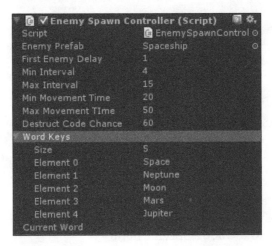

Good, our **Word Keys** array is now set up. Let's return to our
`EnemySpawnController.cs` script and add the following lines
in the `SpawnEnemy()` coroutine at the very end of its `while()` loop:

```
//Create a new empty string for destruct code
string randomCode = "";
//If the random is valid, get a random word
if(Random.Range(0f,100f) < destructCodeChance)
randomCode = GetRandomWord();
//Set the enemy's the DestructCode newEnemy.
SetDestructCode(randomCode);
//Add the enemy to the list of enemies
enemies.Add(newEnemy);
```

When an enemy is initialized, the previous code adds it to the `List` of enemies
and sets its self-destruct code. Now, using the following code, let's create the
`GetRandomWord()` method that will return one of our predefined words:

```
private string GetRandomWord()
{
   //Return a random Word Key
   return wordKeys[Random.Range(0, wordKeys.Length)];
}
```

Good. Some of our enemies have a destruct code assigned. Let's just add a method
to remove an enemy from the `List`, which will be called each time an enemy is
destroyed. The method is added as follows:

```
public void EnemyDestroyed(EnemyController destroyedEnemy)
{
   //Remove the destroyed enemy from the List
   enemies.Remove(destroyedEnemy);
}
```

Open the `EnemyController.cs` script. Within the `Kill()` coroutine, just before
the `Destroy(gameObject)` line, add the following line to remove the enemy from
the `List`:

```
//Remove enemy from the List
EnemySpawnController.instance.EnemyDestroyed(this);
```

Perfect. Save all of the scripts and hit the play button. If you click on an enemy
that has the hacking slider, the hacking process starts and displays a destruct code
when finished.

The last step is to handle the player's input in order to check if he or she types one of
the enemies' self-destruct words.

Handling player input

We will use the Update() method of our EnemySpawnController.cs script to check which characters the player types with his or her keyboard. These characters will be stored one by one and will be compared to our enemies' destruct codes.

Open our EnemySpawnController.cs script and create a new Update() method:

```
void Update()
{
  //If the player has typed a character
  if(!string.IsNullOrEmpty(Input.inputString))
  {
    //Add this new character to the currentWord
    currentWord += Input.inputString;
    //We need to know if the code matches at least 1 enemy
    bool codeMatches = false;
    //Check enemies' destruct codes one by one
    for each(EnemyController enemy in enemies)
    {
      //If the enemy has a destruct code AND is hacked
      if(enemy.destructCode != "" && enemy.hacked)
      {
        //currentWord contain the destruct code?
        if(currentWord.Contains(enemy.destructCode))
        {
          //Yes - Destroy it and update our bool
          StartCoroutine(enemy.Kill());
          codeMatches = true;
        }
      }
    }
    //Did the word match at least 1 enemy?
    if(codeMatches)
    //In that case, reset the currentWord to empty
    currentWord = "";
  }
}
```

Save this script. Now, when you hack an enemy, you can destroy it by typing its self-destruct code! If multiple enemies have the same code, they will be destroyed simultaneously.

Typing a word may scroll the viewport; this is because Q, A, S, and D are set as Horizontal and Vertical axes by default. Go to **Edit | Project Settings | Input** and delete (a, d) and (s, w) from the Horizontal and Vertical axes' Alt Positive Button and Alt Negative Button fields respectively.

Summary

In this chapter, we used everything we learned in the earlier chapters with respect to creating a simple game.

We created an enemy spawning system, which instantiates enemies on the scene. Rigidbodies and colliders have been added to handle collisions between enemies in the barriers at the bottom of the screen.

We also added a health bar widget that is linked to health points; if four enemies touch the end of the screen, the game restarts.

The `Update()` method was used to handle player input and compare the typed word with destruct codes in order to destroy enemies if needed.

For now, the game is quite simple. Some ideas to enhance the game are as follows:

- Add more self-destruct words
- Display what the player types on the screen (visual feedback)
- Slowly increase the spawning rate as the player destroys enemies
- Slowly increase the enemy's speed as the player destroys enemies
- Add a scoring system
- Implement the Time power (hint: Time.timeScale)
- Implement the Bomb power
- Make the hack time depend on barrierCount (more barriers, faster hacking)
- Include the possibility of removing an ActiveBarrier with a right click
- Add clickable objects to regain health; some enemies leave them behind
- Add a combo reward if the player destroys multiple enemies within 3 seconds
- Include harder words for hard difficulty

- Insert a visual indicator (arrow) to show the direction of the enemies outside the screen
- Add more visual variety in the background (galaxies and so on) to help orientation
- Display a game over screen with the main menu and restart buttons
- Create tutorial pop ups

If you add some of the previous features, our game will become more interesting.

In order to improve your knowledge of NGUI, you can refer to more tutorials at `http://www.tasharen.com/forum/index.php?topic=6754`.

The complete NGUI scripting documentation is available at `http://www.tasharen.com/ngui/docs/index.html`.

That's it! We have now finished working with Unity and NGUI using this book. Thank you for your attention and I wish you all the best for your future projects.

Index

Symbols

2D User Interface, NGUI
  creating 10
  parameters, UI Wizard 10
  UI layer, separating 11
  UI Wizard 10
  window, UI Wizard 10

A

ActiveBarrier prefab
  building process 112, 113
  creating 109-111
  events, forwarding to viewport 114
  instantiating 111, 112
Anchor GameObject
  about 17
  parameters 17, 18
animations
  hide options, clipping to 68-71
  smooth powers apparition 68
  using 67
Application.Quit() method 94
Atlas prefab 119
Awake() method 90

B

Barrier availability tool tip
  notifications, setting up 117
BarrierObject cooldown system
  BarrierObject smooth apparition 117
  implementing 115, 116
BarrierRemoved() method 145

BMFont
  about 129
  downloading 129
BuildFinished() method 144
button widget
  about 31
  creating 31
  exit button, adding 33, 34
  parameters 32
  play button, adding 33, 34

C

Camera GameObject
  about 13
  parameters 14-16
C# scripting
  about 79
  events methods 79
  tween methods 84
custom UI structure
  about 11
  anchor 17
  camera 13
  panel 18
  UI Root (2D) 11

D

Damage() method 149
drag-and-drop system
  about 54
  power selection 54
draggable barriers
  BarrierObject prefab, creating 105-107
  creating 104
  dropping, on viewport 107, 108

E

EndOfScreen widget
  creating 149, 150
enemy collisions, handling
  about 144
  active barriers collisions 144-146
  bottom of screen collision 147
  EndOfScreen widget, creating 149
  Healthbar, creating 147, 148
EnemySpawnController.cs script 140
enemy spawning
  about 138
  enemies container, creating 138
  enemy prefab, creating 138, 139
  enemy spawn controller, creating 140, 141
  events, forwarding to viewport 143
error notification 88
events methods
  about 79
  OnClick() method 80
  OnDrag(Vector2 delta) method 80
  OnDrop(GameObject droppedObj)
       method 80
  OnHover(bool state) method 79
  OnInput(string text) method 80
  OnKey(KeyCode key) method 80
  OnPress(bool state) method 79
  OnScroll(float delta) method 80
  OnSelect() method 80
  OnTooltip(bool state) method 80
  OnTooltip() event, creating 81
  tool tip, creating 81
  tool tip, displaying 82, 84
ExitPressed() method 94

F

filled sprite 28
font
  adding 129
  assigning, to Label 132
  creating, in Unity 131
  exporting, BMFont used 129, 130

G

Game atlas
  available powers icons, sprites 122, 123
  creating 120
  font, adding 129
  MainMenu customization 133
  Main Menu window, sliced sprites 127
  selected powers icons, sprites 123, 124
  simple sprites, adding 121
  sliced sprites, adding 125
  sliced sprites, configuring 126, 127
  sprites, adding 120
  tiled sprites, adding 128
game, creating
  enemy collisions, handling 144
  enemy spawning 138
  self-destruct code, creating 150
Game scene
  preparing 97, 98
GetRandomWord() method 157

H

Healthbar
  creating 147
HitByEnemy() method 145

I

image buttons 35

L

label widget
  about 28
  creating 28
  parameters 29
  title bar, creating 29-31
localization system
  about 73
  label, localizing 76
  language selection box 74, 75
  localization component 74
  localization files, creating 74

M

MainMenu customization
performing 133, 134

N

NGUI (Next-Gen User Interface)
about 7
animations 67
atlases 8
Atlas prefab 119
C# scripting 79
drag-and-drop system 54
draggable panel 52
error notification 88-92
events 8
game, creating 137
importing 9
localization 8
localization system 73
scrollable text 72
shaders 9
UIButton Keys component 86
UI, creating 10
widgets 21
Widget Wizard 21
NGUI Professional License 7
NGUI Standard License 7

O

OnClick() method 80
OnDifficultyChange() method 49
OnDrag(Vector2 delta) method 80
OnDrop(GameObject droppedObj)
method 80
OnEnable() method 90
OnHover(bool state) method 79
OnInput(string text) method 80
OnKey(KeyCode key) method 80
OnPress(bool state) method 79
OnScroll(float delta) method 80
OnSelect() method 80
OnTooltip(bool state) method 80
OnTooltip() event 81

OnTriggerEnter() event 144
OnTriggerEnter() method 150
OnVolumeChange() method 42

P

Panel Clipping 68
Panel GameObject
about 18
parameters 18, 19
Pixel Offset parameter 35
PlayerPrefs() method 93
popup list widget
creating 46
difficulty selector, creating 47, 49
parameters 46
powers selection, drag-and-drop system
current item, removing 66
current item, replacing 64, 65
draggable items container, creating 55, 56
draggable items, creating 56- 59
drop surface, creating 59, 60
invalid drop, handling 63
prefabs, creating 60-62

R

RecreateDragItem() method 66

S

Scale Tweens 68
SciFi Atlas
about 22
selecting 22
scrollable text
about 72
creating 72, 73
scrollable viewport
about 97
building 97, 98
draggable background 99
keyboard scrolling 103, 104
scroll bars, linking 100-102
self-destruct code
adding, localization files 153
assigning, to enemy 154

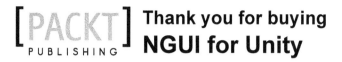

About Packt Publishing

Packt, pronounced 'packed', published its first book "*Mastering phpMyAdmin for Effective MySQL Management*" in April 2004 and subsequently continued to specialize in publishing highly focused books on specific technologies and solutions.

Our books and publications share the experiences of your fellow IT professionals in adapting and customizing today's systems, applications, and frameworks. Our solution based books give you the knowledge and power to customize the software and technologies you're using to get the job done. Packt books are more specific and less general than the IT books you have seen in the past. Our unique business model allows us to bring you more focused information, giving you more of what you need to know, and less of what you don't.

Packt is a modern, yet unique publishing company, which focuses on producing quality, cutting-edge books for communities of developers, administrators, and newbies alike. For more information, please visit our website: www.packtpub.com.

Writing for Packt

We welcome all inquiries from people who are interested in authoring. Book proposals should be sent to author@packtpub.com. If your book idea is still at an early stage and you would like to discuss it first before writing a formal book proposal, contact us; one of our commissioning editors will get in touch with you.

We're not just looking for published authors; if you have strong technical skills but no writing experience, our experienced editors can help you develop a writing career, or simply get some additional reward for your expertise.

Unity 4.x Cookbook

ISBN: 978-1-84969-042-3   Paperback: 386 pages

Over 100 recipes to spice up your Unity skills

1. A wide range of topics are covered, ranging in complexity, offering something for every Unity 4 game developer

2. Every recipe provides step-by-step instructions, followed by an explanation of how it all works, and alternative approaches or refinements

3. Book developed with the latest version of Unity (4.x)

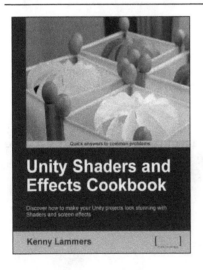

Unity Shaders and Effects Cookbook

ISBN: 978-1-84969-508-4   Paperback: 268 pages

Discover how to make your Unity projects look stunning with Shaders and screen effects

1. Learn the secrets of creating AAA quality Shaders without having to write long algorithms

2. Add realism to your game with stunning Screen Effects

3. Understand the structure of Surface Shaders through easy to understand step-by-step examples

Please check **www.PacktPub.com** for information on our titles

Unity for Architectural Visualization

ISBN: 978-1-78355-906-0   Paperback: 144 pages

Transform your architectural design into an interactive real-time experience using Unity

1. Simple instructions to help you set up an interactive and real-time scene

2. Excellent tips on making your presentations attractive by creating interactive designs

3. Most important features of computer games covered, to develop compelling, interactive scenes for so-called "serious games"

Unity 4.x Game AI Programming

ISBN: 978-1-84969-340-0   Paperback: 232 pages

Learn and implement game AI in Unity3D with a lot of sample projects and next-generation techniques to use in your Unity3D projects

1. A practical guide with step-by-step instructions and example projects to learn Unity3D scripting

2. Learn pathfinding using A* algorithms as well as Unity3D pro features and navigation graphs

3. Implement finite state machines (FSMs), path following, and steering algorithms

Please check **www.PacktPub.com** for information on our titles

www.ingramcontent.com/pod-product-compliance
Lightning Source LLC
Chambersburg PA
CBHW060134060326
40690CB00018B/3875